BE BOLD

HOW TO PREPARE YOUR HEART AND MIND FOR RACIAL RECONCILIATION

LATOYA J. BURRELL

HIGH BRIDGE BOOKS
HOUSTON

Dedication

This book is dedicated to my husband, Greg, my brother, Justin, and my two sons, Grayson and Garrison. May they be seen by their hearts and not judged by the color of their skin. This book is also dedicated to the memory of everyone who lost their lives, prematurely, to the system. Finally, this book is dedicated to everyone who is on the journey to becoming BOLD!

Your Journey to Being Bold

Introduction

*From everyone who has been given much, much will
be demanded; and from the one who has been entrusted with much, much more will be asked.*

—Luke 12:48

God is truly at work when you begin to have sleepless
nights because your mind is consumed with the work to be
done. As we closed out the first and entered the second
quarter of 2020, our world was shaken by the pandemic
that changed life as we know it. Adjusting to the new norm
included zoom calls, homeschooling, limitations on gatherings, and simply watching the daily news reporting of the
statistics of rising cases. It seemed like we were leaving a
season of temporarily sheltering in place to the new norm
of social distancing.

Then our world was rocked when George Floyd was
murdered after a police officer, sworn to protect and serve,
kept his knee on Mr. Floyd's neck for eight minutes and
forty-six seconds. This sparked national, then global uproar
as people took to the streets to protest in not only every single state in America but in over sixty countries across the
world.

Why, now, are so many people of all races, ages, reli-
gions, and socio-economic statuses coming together? What

can I do? How can I be an ally? How can I have the uncomfortable conversation about race? The questions continued to come, but for the first time in my life, my response was different. I felt the call to action and the need to do something.

In the past, I felt that it was not my responsibility to educate everyone else! I would often say it is not my job to be the black voice or spokesperson for an entire race. While I do believe that statement to be true, I also feel that I have more of a responsibility than to just be silent. Silence speaks volumes and can sometimes be viewed as being complicit. Do I agree with the racial injustices and mishaps occurring? The answer is a resounding No! Do I want to be complicit? Absolutely not. Not speaking up was also somewhat sparked by the fear of being misunderstood and ultimately risking what I have worked hard for. Silence was safe.

The American dream suggests that the path to happiness and success is to get an education and work hard. Then and only then can you have access to even the smallest piece of the American pie, the white picket fence, and other luxuries associated with that dream. I somehow associated using my voice as possibly compromising the very things I have worked hard for.

What would others think? What if I compromise myself, my job, my position, status, or relationships? I do not want to compromise attaining the American dream by speaking about anything taboo. I am reminded of this as I observe the cancel culture hashtag and movement, whereby celebrities are #cancelled for doing or saying something deemed offensive. What is the solution to avoid compromising yourself? Tread lightly with your comments … Remain quiet.

In addition to not wanting to compromise my access to the dream or my comfort, I was often quiet because I did not want to be viewed as an angry black woman. I was reminded of this when I read a post scrolling through Facebook during the immediate aftermath of the death of George Floyd. The post said, "I have often been the quiet black girl in hope of not being viewed as the angry black woman." Wow, I echoed the sentiment of the author of the post ... *no more!* No more being quiet at the risk of being viewed as angry. No more being quiet to ensure that I and others remained comfortable. No more not speaking up when the truth is warranted.

Also, something was different about George Floyd's death. Yes, we have seen and heard police dash camera footage related to previous killings of unarmed black people. But this time, we were able to see the police officer face to face. We were able to look this killer directly in his eyes and watch his conscious and intentional movements as he moved his knee back and forward over George Floyd's neck. The world was able to look him in his eyes and see it. The world was able to witness George Floyd take his last breath.

The day after George Floyd's Houston funeral, I had a text exchange with two of my good girlfriends. One of them was sitting in her corporate business meeting, where the topic was ... yes, you guessed it, what can we do? She expressed to me that she did not want to have to educate everyone about race. She also confirmed that she prefers that the diversity trainer be a person of color from outside of the organization. She added, "I don't want to lead the discussion, but I do want my voice to be heard."

I said, "Well, it sounds like you believe that we also must do some educating and be the change that we want to see." I know what my friend meant because I share the sentiment. I know that the one seminar or training is not enough, and because I, like my colleagues, am not a certified diversity trainer, I do not want to be presumed to be the leader of the pack when our designated diversity trainer completes the initial training. I simply want my non-black colleagues to commit to the same open-minded level of learning about race and racism that I have committed to throughout my life.

The default is to expect the people of color to automatically serve on diversity-related task forces and speak to issues or topics related to diversity and inclusion. Despite not wanting to be viewed as the leader of the pack, I have changed my mind and decided, *Why not lead the discussion and efforts?* Why not be the bridge to get others in my sphere of influence past the discomfort of talking about race?

So whose job is it to "fix" racism and lead the charge toward racial reconciliation? Frankly, we *all* have a part to play. It is interesting that, overnight, our country went from sheltering in place to flooding the streets in protest — protesting to end racial injustices, which stem from what has consumed America since its inception, the ugly R-word ... *racism*!

Regardless of the how or why, the point is we are here. Whether we thought America was post-racial or whether we believe race is a social construct, the very actions taking place around the country suggest that we may not be post-racial after all. Whether a social construct or not, race has power.

Introduction

Maybe I, too, am like the many Americans who for the first time was forced to slow down my daily grind due to COVID-19. No more jam-packed schedules, no commutes, no sports, no gyms, no restaurants, and ultimately, fewer distractions. Because of the fewer distractions, many of us seemingly had more time ... time to listen, time to dream, time to make a difference. Some may even call it divine intervention. God slowed life down to open our eyes. Lord, you have our attention!

In the midst of a pandemic, silence was broken and COVID-19 became an afterthought. When the coronavirus came in like a thief in the night, I witnessed the daily news consumption shift from 24-7 reporting of swiftly rising COVID-19 numbers, to outrage over the country remaining closed, and then to the heartbreak over the unemployment numbers and COVID-related deaths.

People could not bury their loved ones in the traditional sense. Drive-through and Facebook Live funerals became common. But suddenly, something was larger than COVID. Is racism so bad in America that people would seemingly forget that we are in the middle of a "deadly" pandemic? Is it so bad that people were willing to risk their lives, literally, at the risk of not standing up to ensure that justice is served? It began to feel like we now had two pandemics, one being racism. It felt like one pandemic required masks, while the other required an unmasking.

While it seemed that the country was coming together, I was reminded that we, in fact, were divided. As the protests began, my heart broke daily, as I would get on social media, read and watch the news, and continually be reminded that our country is not only divided but broken. Now don't mistake me when I say the country is broken.

Our country was never whole, but it doesn't change the fact that the broken country is hurting. The broken country is tired. The broken country seems ready for a change, almost 400 years since the Transatlantic slave trade.

In addition, I see the constant tweets from politicians, the many anti-Black Lives Matter or George Floyd hateful and racist posts on social media, and the supporting comments that defend the hateful and racist posts. Of course, I am aware of the First Amendment and its speech-related protections. I also know that my not agreeing with someone does not make them wrong. But let's be clear—the posts and many supporting comments were purely racist. They spewed hate and division.

Being a harmonizer, and wanting to see the best in people, my only alternative view is that while racist, these comments perhaps are from uneducated or uninformed people. In the literal sense, they are ignorant of the true nature of race relations. Maybe they have heard about slavery, but do they really know the full context, scope, and monstrous magnitude? Maybe they do not know the love of Christ? I considered quoting some of those hurtful and hateful posts but decided to preserve the positive energy I hope to exude within the two covers of this book and not give a platform to the ignorance.

To give minimal context, these comments were from teachers, business professionals, and students heading to universities, including Christian universities. They were a slap in the face and a reminder that, unfortunately, we may never see a time where racism is completely non-existent. After all, racism is a matter of the heart. Racism is taught. Racism is a sin problem. Sin will always be a problem. But I remind myself that even though racism will likely always persist with some, that doesn't mean it has to remain acceptable or tolerated. It doesn't mean we can't attempt to dismantle racism and put a stop to systematic oppression. It does not mean we cannot or should not work toward racial reconciliation. To put a stop to systematic oppression, we have to continue to apply pressure and become educated about how and why systematic oppression remains an issue in 2020. In the famous 1963 "Letter from a Birmingham Jail," Dr. Martin Luther King Jr. said the following:

> We know through painful experience that freedom is never voluntarily given by the oppressor; it must be demanded by the oppressed. Frankly, I have yet to engage in a direct action campaign that was "well timed" in the view of those who have not suffered unduly from the disease of segregation.

Almost sixty years later, this statement still rings true. The comments and actions caused me to think long and hard about the role the church has in the wake of this second pandemic, the pandemic of racism. Whose job is it to fix this problem? This is not about politics. In fact, all political parties are imperfect. This is not to blame a certain party or individual!

Politics keep us divided. This problem is bigger than any political party! Politics is something to hide behind. The problem is spiritual, related to our hearts, minds, and souls. Thankfully, no problem is too big for our God. Philippians 4:6 states, "Do not be anxious about anything, but in every situation, by prayer and petition, with thanksgiving, present your requests to God."

I believe in the power of prayer! My prayer and petition is that we can get to a place where our world looks more like Heaven! My prayer is that every person reading this book can expand their hearts and minds and find and exude peace and love.

1

My Call to Action

*And as we let our own light shine, we uncon-
sciously give other people permission to do the same.
As we are liberated from our own fear, our presence
automatically liberates others.*

—Marianne Williamson

Living and working in Minneapolis, Minnesota, I was in the center of the uproar. The day after George Floyd was killed and the video went viral, I was walking home with my family from the Commons Park across from US Bank Stadium, which is five blocks away from our downtown Minneapolis home. As we neared our home, my husband began to rub his eyes and said his eyes were burning. I immediately agreed that mine were likewise burning. We were walking by a new construction site, so I presumed it was some chemical used on the new project.

As we got home and turned on the news, we learned of protestors being tear-gassed, literally 2.5 miles away from our home. I immediately told my husband that burning we felt in our eyes was tear gas. If we felt it 2.5 miles away, can you imagine the point-blank range impact? What could these protestors have done so bad that warranted tear gas? What else was to come?

In the immediate days to follow, we visited the crime scene—now a large community gathering and mourning place—observed the beautiful artistic expressions, and witnessed the growing mural space. We visited the Third Police precinct and saw the charcoal remains. We also observed the immediate clean-up efforts.

We attended a protest, heard protestors daily, heard choppers, and witnessed the 18-wheeler drive into a crowd, a crowd where I knew many attendees. Daily calls and texts from family and friends around the country to check on our safety and well-being reminded me that this issue was larger than Minneapolis. This issue was, seemingly, larger than George Floyd.

Fast-forward almost two weeks and hundreds of protests later, there are many discussions to be had—a lot of uncertainty. But one thing is certain … times are changing, and people are tired of the same results. Living in the midst of it all was only the tip of the iceberg. North Central University, where I currently work and serve, was asked to host the Minneapolis George Floyd Memorial. I was invited to attend. I have been asked, "How did it feel to be in the memorial? What was the energy like in the room?"

During the memorial, our University President made a charge to university presidents around the world, to establish a George Floyd Memorial Scholarship fund. The story was written about in *Forbes* and reported on by many other large news outlets. His message was heard across the world as the memorial was streamed live nationwide. After the memorial, President Hagan confirmed that his message was not staged … It was all God. The scholarship call from President Hagan led to many universities accepting the call to create George Floyd Memorial Scholarships.

During the memorial, I opted to sit in the back row of the sanctuary, which was only about ten rows back due to the intimate size of the first level of the sanctuary. I observed Minneapolis Mayor Jacob Frey kneel before the casket and break into tears. I watched Governor Tim Waltz enter and be greeted by other politicians, some local and some who flew in for this occasion.

I watched a few celebrities enter the room with the Floyd family, including Reverend Al Sharpton, scheduled to deliver the eulogy. I watched the media maneuver the room and quietly digested this event, which felt more like a private social gathering, as we all wore VIP lanyards with Floyd's photograph under the letters VIP. All of this as the golden closed casket sat front and center and Floyd's photo projected on the large overhead screen.

With masks on, and as a result of the social distancing guidelines, we were required to skip a seat between us and our neighbor. I sat in one seat, to my immediate right was my husband, and to my immediate left was the police chief, Medaria Arradondo. Chief Arradondo, the first African American to serve on the Minneapolis Police Department[1], was the chief of the four officers arrested for the murder of George Floyd.

Days before the memorial, I heard him on the news boldly state that the silence and inaction of the three other officers suggested complicit behavior. My heart ached for the Floyd family, but my heart also ached for this man. As he sat there, he was seemingly hesitant to clap or move. I saw the media within the sanctuary capture photos of him, some openly and some discretely.

Leading up to the memorial, I felt compelled to do more. I felt a call of action, which was amplified after the memorial as I watched Floyd's casket be pushed out of the chapel and into the hearse. Being a person who values accountability, I decided to record my very first Facebook Live video that same day. I confessed my sense of conviction and my acceptance of the call to action I felt.

This video was accountability for me. I immediately engulfed myself in the cause—reading, watching, and listening—and before the next Tuesday, the day of Floyd's official Houston funeral, I had already immersed myself in writing this book. I accepted and continue to accept the call to action, which, for me, includes doing more, using my voice, and being a bridge toward racial reconciliation.

The day after attending the Floyd Memorial, I attended a prayer meeting at North Central University, in the same sanctuary the Floyd Memorial was held in on the previous day. One of the speakers quoted Joshua 1:9: "Have I not commanded you? Be strong and courageous. Do not be afraid; do not be discouraged, for the Lord your God will be with you wherever you go."

I immediately texted a colleague and friend in the room and said, "Who is he, because I believe that message is for me." Wow, can it be any clearer? So that weekend, I prayed and studied the book of Joshua. Following the memorial and prayer meeting, I reflected on how uncomfortable I was with everything going on around me. 2020 had been far from comfortable. COVID-19, changes at work due to social distancing and closures, virtual learning for nine weeks with my kindergartner coupled with having my twenty-two-month-old son at home, all while balancing work.

I am not complaining ... I am blessed. I have my health, a job, food, shelter, and my family, but I can't deny the discomfort. I know that God sometimes calls us to be uncomfortable. I did not think that in 2020, I would be taking my six-year-old son to a protest, explaining police brutality, or having a discussion with him about racism, yet here we are. With mixed emotions, I am having many discussions with colleagues who do not look like me. I am constantly being asked by neighbors, friends, and family, "What can I do?" What should I tell them?

I am no stranger to race relations. I am from the deep South, born and raised in Louisiana. I can say one thing with certainty ... racism persists in Louisiana, and most Louisiana natives are upfront and direct. People, both black and white, are open and honest if they don't like someone of another race.

Louisiana is very black and white—either you are black or white, with not much in between for diversity in race. If your skin is black or of color, you are categorized as black. If your skin is white, despite being a member of a minority group, you are more inclined to be associated as white. The exception to that unwritten, but well-exercised, rule would be the minority with white skin choosing to self-associate with black people. As shallow as it may seem, that was my experience and reality for the first thirty years of my life— no true exposure to diversity beyond black and white, but certainly exposure to racism, bias, and prejudices.

Despite my background and all the discomfort issued in with 2020, I decided to step out of my comfort zone. The day before I began writing this book, I recorded a short eleven-minute YouTube video entitled "Here is what you can do" and in response to the question I explained the following four things that you can do:

1. Examine Yourself and Your Heart
2. Educate Yourself (Learn)
3. Humble Yourself (Listen)
4. Be Bold

The overwhelming response confirmed that this book was not only necessary but that it was my job to be the author. I knew it was my time to be *bold*. In the weeks to follow, I found myself second-guessing if I would be misunderstood in writing this well-intentioned book. After prayer, I knew I could not allow fear to suffocate my voice. I could not let fear banish my boldness.

As we are living in these turbulent times, resulting from the double pandemic impacting our world, people are anxious to get back to normal. They want to return to moving about the world without masks and the need for social distancing. But what if God did not intend for us to go back to normal? What if his plan is for us to come out of this pandemic, better, stronger, and bolder?

I am reminded of the following Peter Drucker quote: "[t]he greatest danger in times of turbulence is not the turbulence; it is to act with yesterday's logic."[2] If you keep doing what you have been doing, you will keep getting what you have been getting. Perhaps the greatest problem facing us is not racism itself but the logic or response we give to the topic. I am encouraged that if we shift the discussions, change the focus, and redirect our actions and reactions, we may make significant strides in our quest for racial reconciliation. I have to change my logic. My voice matters, it is my job, and I can no longer act and react with yesterday's logic. I must be obedient. I must be bold! So here we go!

2

The Road Map for This Journey

No one is born hating another person because of the color of his skin, or his background, or his religion. People must learn to hate, and if they can learn to hate, they can be taught to love, for love comes more naturally to the human heart than its opposite.

—Nelson Mandela

My goal for this book is to begin the open and honest dialogue needed to help everyone have tough discussions about race and racism. I encourage everyone to take the following four steps: Examine your heart, listen, learn, and ultimately, *be bold!* We must be the change we want to see.

It is not a one-time effort. It is not just attending one conference, one seminar, or having one discussion. While all of those are valuable, the process is cyclical. This book will get you started on these four steps. The goal at the end of the book is for you to be bold as you continue to listen and learn and bring others along on this journey with you.

First Step Toward Being Bold

I encourage you to identify a group of peers, coworkers, family members, or others who are also boldly interested in becoming agents for change. This group will be known as your Growth Group! You should plan to journey through this book with your Growth Group. Whether it be one or ten others, whether it be your spouse or colleagues, your friends, or church members, get you a group to do life with, starting with this book.

I also encourage you to get a diverse group, where possible. Genuinely create diverse relationships. These relationships lead to conversing. Conversing leads to understanding, which allows growth. We must change our mindset and be willing to expand our circles, which ultimately may become feeders to our Growth Groups. To love our neighbors, we must know them. To know them, we must be willing to engage with them. To have this willingness to engage, we must be willing to change our mindset.

Once you identify this Growth Group, you are ready! If you don't have a group, don't be discouraged. You can read the book alone, but my prayer is that you will want to further discuss many of these topics with others and feel bold enough to do so at the proper time. As you embark on this journey, you will have to examine your heart. Examining your heart is personal, but in this book, we will briefly discuss some foundation on why your heart matters and how your heart ultimately allows you to love, listen, and learn.

For listen and learn, this book explores brief American history from the lens of the African American experience, the different stages of racial reconciliation, and the top ten questions continuously raised as it relates to race or racism.

In addition to providing a brief response to each question, there are Dialogue Questions for you to dig deeper with in your Growth Group. These responses are not designed to be exhaustive, and there is room for you to further research these topics.

We live in the information age. While digging deeper with your Growth Group, do additional research on the question or topic. After all, learning often includes research. I assure you, there are many free resources, YouTube videos, podcasts, TED Talks, books, movies, and articles that further expound on every topic! This book will end with specific tips on how to continue to be bold.

Before the first discussion with your Growth Group, I challenge you to take a pretest! Yes, I am an educator through and through. Good news, this one isn't for a grade! You will pass, as long as you follow the one rule: *Be honest with yourself!*

Note that the pretest requires openness. I don't mean that the pretest is open book, but instead open heart ... Please take the test with an open heart. Take some time to reflect on the following questions, write down your answers, and then schedule some time to discuss them with your Growth Group.

No Grade Pretest

1. When is the first time you were stopped by a cop? Do you recall details about the stop?
2. Have you ever had a teacher who was not your race? When was it? How did you feel?
3. Do you recall your first time talking about race? When was it? Who was it with?

4. Do you remember your first friend of another race? Were they welcome to your home or birthday parties?
5. Have you ever been the minority at school or work? If yes, how did that make you feel?
6. Does talking about race make you uncomfortable? Why?
7. Do you believe that white privilege exists? If yes, have you personally experienced it?
8. Do you have anyone of another race in your immediate family? If yes, do you view that family member as different?
9. Have you ever been the victim of racism? When? How did it make you feel?
10. Are you racist? How does this question make you feel?

That was an easy pretest, right? Now, these questions aren't to convict you, make you feel guilty, or make you defensive. They are designed to be eye-openers.

I vividly recall my first time being stopped by a cop. I was in college, taking my four-hour drive from my home to my college town in Natchitoches, Louisiana. I was pulled over on 1-49N, between Alexandria and Natchitoches. The cop was extra rude, making me get out of my car, and I felt scared because I was being stopped as it was getting dark outside.

I was certain that I was not speeding, as my cruise control was set. After questioning me about where I was headed, he said my taillight was out. I had no idea. He gave me a ticket. I drove away with a pounding heart, wondering why he was so mean.

I worked at a clothing store in my college town, and during the Christmas holiday, the store carried holiday décor. One day, a white woman and her son came into the store, and the little boys noticed a black Santa. He said to his mother, "Momma, I never knew Santa was a N*gg*r." The entire store got quiet. She quickly yanked the little boy and told him to shut his mouth. Why now was she embarrassed? After all, the little boy had to learn this behavior somewhere, right? What did that child's first discussion about racism look like?

I also vividly recall my first discussions about race and the various talks that had to reassure me that I was pretty, smart, and deserving. I was frequently reminded of how my blackness would cause me to have to work harder, be seen in a different light, and sometimes, perhaps not treated the same.

I have had with my younger brother the talk about what to do and not to do when stopped by a police officer. I still experience anxiety when stopped by a cop. I have generally been not only the minority but the only black woman in school and work settings. I am well aware of the phrase "token black person"! And yes, talking about race also makes me uncomfortable! So that's a little glimpse into my pretest!

None of our pretests will likely escape some remnant of racial implications. You see, racism is so embedded in the fabric of America's quilt. Unfortunately, it's intertwined in the essence of who we are. Race and racism are not a white person problem. The feeling of discomfort also exists in non-white people. Use the pretest as a personal context to determine where you are now and where you want to be. The pretest was not designed to cause guilt but, instead, awareness and accountability.

While some people do not believe that racism is real, others suggest it is a social construct. My stance is, whether intentional or not, the impact of racism is undeniable. Further, even if race is a social construct, the construct is powerful and real. Racism is real. Racism is taught. Racism can equate to hate. Love is real. Love is needed to trump racism. Racism can be very personal because the feelings and experiences are often very personal. I invite you to reflect on your own experiences. Are you ready to continue this journey?

3

Examine Yourself

Above all else, guard your heart, for everything you do flows from it.

—Proverbs 4:23

You cannot hide your heart. Whatever fills, spills.

—Scott Hagan

Many books and resources examine and explore matters of the heart. I am not a medical doctor, but I know enough about anatomy to understand how essential the heart is to our natural existence. Many emotions are tied to the heart— one of the most common being love. The best love story I have ever read is the Bible! It's a book about redemption and, overall, God's love. In fact, we are commanded to love:

> Teacher, which is the greatest commandment in the Law? Jesus replied: "'Love the Lord your God with all your heart and with all your soul

and with all your mind." This is the first and greatest commandment. And the second is like it: 'Love your neighbor as yourself.' All the Law and the Prophets hang on these two commandments. (Matt. 22:36-40)

Loving God may come easy, but what about loving everyone else? Why do we need racial reconciliation? If the Bible tells us to love our neighbor, why do people often not love all of their neighbors? How do you love your neighbor? Which neighbor requires love? In the literal sense, is this your physical residential neighbor only or everyone? Is it only those neighbors who look like you? Only those neighbors you choose to engage with? Only those neighbors you are comfortable with?

History and segregation have made following this simplistic and straightforward commandment complicated. Is this complication powerful enough to cause us to ignore this commandment? We must acknowledge this barrier and declare that it is a problem. Then and only then can we take steps toward complete reconciliation. Scripture is clear: *Thou shalt love the Lord thy God with all thy heart, and with all thy soul, and with all thy mind.* We must love with *all* of our heart, soul, and mind, not just a fraction, so we ought to make sure that our whole heart, our whole soul, and our whole mind are pure!

Many scriptures address the need to examine and guard our hearts. According to Strong's Exhaustive Concordance, the word *heart* is stated in Scripture 826 times (more often in other translations).[3] While the Bible does not give a direct definition of what the heart is, the context used heavily suggests that the reference is beyond just associations with the vital organ in our body, necessary for life.

The heart, in the biblical sense, relates to our emotions and desires, feelings, thoughts, actions, inactions, and morals. The heart is emotional. The heart is spiritual. The Hebrew definition of *heart* references the mind and thoughts,[4] and the inner part of a person, and refers to our will, mind, consciousness, emotion, and understanding.

As stated, Proverbs 4:23 tells us to guard our hearts. Different translations use different words, but the summation is that the heart is the spring well for life. Another translation says out of the heart comes the issues of life. I believe this to be true. Before you can truly get to a place of racial reconciliation, you must examine and ensure that your heart and mind are pure.

But the fruit of the Spirit is love, joy, peace, forbearance, kindness, goodness, faithfulness, gentleness and self-control. Against such things there is no law.

—Galatians 5:22-23

When examining my own heart and assuring that I am keeping a pure heart, I remind myself of the fruit of the Spirit. It's a guide and accountability in ensuring that I keep a pure heart, because to display and walk in the fruit of the Spirit, I must love. Galatians 5 is a model of how I want to live my life at all times.

Understanding that I am saved by the grace of God, I am motivated to keep my heart pure and let my actions reflect that of Galatians 5. I walk in peace, knowing that I have freedom, and try to let my actions reflect the heart of someone who is saved. I also rest in knowing that my actions are not an effort in hopes of gaining salvation, but my actions are reflections of the fact that I am saved. Jesus paid the ultimate price on the cross, and my life is one of humble thanksgiving.

If I cannot love all people, despite our differences … if I cannot have a heart and mind open to seeking racial reconciliation, it's a direct stance against loving my neighbor as myself. How can I love my neighbor if I do not know them? How can I love my neighbor if I have biases and prejudices against them? According to 1 John 4:20, "Whoever claims to love God yet hates a brother or sister is a liar. For whoever does not love their brother and sister, whom they have seen, cannot love God, whom they have not seen."

I am reminded of who I belong to, and as a child of God, I am committed to knowing and loving all of my brothers and sisters in Christ, not in the lens that I want to see them in but in the image that God created them in. Finally, loving with all of my heart, mind, and soul includes acceptance of his creations, loving all of his children, and keeping the Matthew 22:36-40 commandment in its entirety.

In examining yourself, I also encourage you to be honest with yourself about any remnants of the spirits of hatred or racism that may be present. The first step is admitting that something unfavorable may be taking up space. The next step is to call that spirit by its name and pray for its removal.

Declare that you don't want hatred and racism to occupy space in your life or your heart. Declutter that space in your heart. The opposite of love is hate. If there is hate in any part of your heart, it is impossible to love with your whole heart. Racism or biases are problems if you allow them to remain problems. We must soften our hearts. If you don't want biases to persist, take ownership and control, and make the changes necessary. Further, just because you do not hate does not mean that you are displaying love. Love requires action and intentionality. Take steps to intentionally demonstrate love. Make love an action and not something to be reflected by the so-called inaction of hate.

In his famous "Love in Action" sermon, Dr. Martin Luther King Jr. said, "One day we will learn that the heart can never be totally right if the head is totally wrong. Only through bringing together the head and heart—intelligence and goodness—shall man rise to fulfillment of his true nature."[5] Your goal is to get to a place where your heart and mind are in sync!

In addition to examining your heart, I encourage you to examine yourself. Create a strategic development plan for your life. Get a journal and reflect on your life. In addition to the plan, I encourage you to write a mission statement for your life. Yes, I know you are not an organization, but I encourage you to adopt some tools that organizations use to organize their governance and be successful.

How do you want to govern yourself? If you want to be a better you, if you want to have a better, purer heart, I encourage you to take time to reflect on what your true purpose in life is. Now, of course, many will say the ultimate purpose is the Great Commission as stated in Mark 16:15, "He said to them, 'Go into all the world and preach the gospel to all creation.'"

The good news is sharing the gospel, which is that Jesus died on the cross for our sins. In doing this, you are making disciples. But how can you disciple someone if you don't first understand who and whose you are? How can you disciple others if you are not willing to cross the racial line and engage with others who don't look like you?

How can you go and disciple the nations when you do not feel comfortable talking to your domestic neighbors who do not look like you? I like the analogy of putting your own oxygen mask on first, as flight attendants often tell us when we fly. After all, if you aren't secure, how can you help others?

My mission in life is not merely to survive, but to thrive; and to do so with some passion, some compassion, some humor, and some style.

—Maya Angelou

In addition to writing a mission statement of what you want your life to reflect, I encourage you to also write a vision and value statement for your life. Many free resources can challenge you to think about your mission, vision, values, and overall plan! I encourage you to explore.

Another exercise is to get yourself a board of directors. Your board should include influential people in your life, who you seek counsel from before making major decisions or just in general to guide you during your life. The board may be compromised of a parent, spouse, teacher, co-worker, supervisor, or friend. I encourage you to pray about who should be on your entrusted board of directors. There is not a set number of seats for your board nor are there any terms for the years of service. Do what is best for you.

Invest time in developing and becoming a better and stronger you. I encourage you to use the next page to begin drafting a mission, vision, and values statement and listing potential board members. Remember, whatever you water will grow, so intentionally feed and water your soul with positivity.

Your Personal Reflections

Your Mission:

Your Vision:

Your Values:

Your Board of Directors:

1.
2.
3.
4.
5.
6.
7.
8.

Now that you have drafted your mission, vision, values statements, and listed potential board members, I encourage you to discuss the content with your Growth Group.

4

Your Story

The story of your life is not your life; it's your story.

—John Barth

One of the most awkward questions in any job inter-view is "Tell me about yourself?" This is a challenging question. What do they want to know? How far back should I go? What is enough? What is too much? Why is this such a challenging question? After all, we do know ourselves, right?

After your pretest, reflect on your story. Some of the components of our stories are out of our control. We do not control when we are born, where we are born, to whom we are born, or the conditions we are dealt—good or bad. We do not choose the color of our skin! But God makes no mistakes. His intentions were for *you*, yes you, to be you—born in that time, in that place, to those parents, in that skin. His intention was for us all to live in such a time as this.

Before you can grow, lead, change, and Be Bold, you must understand who you are. Part of that challenge for me was first understanding who I belong to, and that allowed me to frame my heart, purpose, mission, and commission! I challenge you to think about your story. Take some time and think about what makes you who you are today.

I like to view my life as chapters. As we know, a book can have multiple chapters, and the content in those chapters differ—some long and some short. Some chapters will be good and others may be great. Some may be shameful and overall bad, while some may be neutral and others have a turn and become great. The compilation of the chapters should be viewed holistically. Rarely are the chapters viewed in isolation. In fact, it's a challenge to tell a story without looking at the full context of all chapters. Your life is like a book. There are different chapters, and they add to who you are but do not define who you are.

I was introduced to a lifeline exercise a few years ago. I have continued to use it in classes and in personal circles. It's a tool that aids you in really reflecting on and sharing your story. I encourage you to take a few minutes to complete the lifeline exercise, located in the next chapter. After completing it, discuss your lifeline with your Growth Group.

A part of examining yourself is exploring your story, sharing your story, and hearing others' life stories. As you complete your lifeline, please share your experiences with your Growth Group and listen to the stories of others. After you complete your lifeline, I will share my story. Listening to the stories of others is an early and important step in this process and leads to courageous conversations.

5

Your Lifeline

The more you praise and celebrate your life, the more there is in life to celebrate.

—Oprah Winfrey

The purpose of the lifeline exercise is to explore your

life from your earliest memory to the present day, highlighting the high and low points. The lifeline is a tool to aid you in becoming more self-aware. In one of my favorite books, *Discover Your True North*, author Bill George states that authentic leaders must be self-aware. Self-awareness is defined as "the ability to see yourself clearly and objectively through reflection and introspection."[6]

Lifeline Exercise Directions

A blank lifeline is included in this chapter. Let me explain the directions for completing it. You are to go down the line, adding pivotal times in your life from birth to the present day. The experiences should be in chronological order. If you deem the experience to be positive, write it on the left side, and if you believe it to be negative, write it on the right side. If it's neutral, write it on the line. Though not required, I encourage you to put the really great things to the far far left and the really negative experiences to the far right.

Imagine that there is an invisible axis of 1-10 running horizontally across the page. The line itself would be the 5 point of the axis. The far left would be a 1 on the axis (the best experience ever) and the far right would be a 10 on the axis (the worst experience ever). If it's between 1 and 5, overall good, write it on the left, and if between 5 and 10, overall negative, write it on the right.

You choose what matters and gets space on your life-line. Common examples include milestones such as births and deaths of others, graduations and other accomplishments, new jobs, major moves, and whatever else you think had an impact on the trajectory of your life. Now, brothers and sisters, you were made on purpose, and it's positive. God makes no mistakes, so I took the liberty of placing your birthday on the line for you, at the very top! Happy Exploring!

My Lifeline

Positive

Adverse

My Birthday

Post Lifeline Reflections

After completing the lifeline exercise, reflect on the following questions:

1. What is your overall takeaway?

2. What are the common themes?

3. What are commonalities with the positive experiences?

4. What are commonalities with the adverse experiences?

5. What is one major thing you learned about yourself?

When I reflect on my life, I don't know what chapters are coming, but I do know what the final chapter holds. I find peace in knowing that in the end, my final chapter will be victorious. That alone makes me want to do more because I know that being saved by the Grace of God makes me want to be a reflection of who God designed me to be. I want to be a reflection of the Love of Christ.

When we die, it is common for our obituaries to have the date we were born, a dash, then the date that we die. Though only one small dash, for many, it represents eight or nine decades of life. I want to ensure that the "dash" of my life is filled with positivity and that I can leave my mark.

My first time completing the lifeline exercise, I was in the legal continuing education class with a group of women lawyers. We were asked to partner with a neighbor to discuss our completed lifelines. The odd thing is it was sharing your heart with a stranger. For some, this may be easier than sharing with your Growth Group because your Growth Group likely includes people you frequently interact with, but the stranger is someone you may never see again.

I don't recall the name of the young woman I partnered with. I shared my lifeline, and despite seemingly negative things, I had them and everything else on the positive side. While in that moment they may have seemed adverse, I know that God put me in those situations for a reason, and in hindsight, I can see the lessons from those occurrences.

We were encouraged to share, and my partner insisted that I share first, to which I obliged. After I shared, she said, "I don't feel comfortable sharing now because I feel like a complaining whiner." She was a white female, born of married parents who both were college professors. Her worst experience, which she plotted on the adverse side, was when she was thirteen years old and her parents moved her family to another state for jobs at a University.

Although I did not compare our stories, my lifeline revealed that my teenage parents were not married when I was born and that I was the firstborn and a first-generation college student. Although I don't think those two facts made me inferior, she seemed to suggest that if I could have had a "harder" life and not complain, what gives her the right? She told me she felt guilty because I saw those seemingly negative experiences as overall positive.

This thirty-something-year-old, college-educated lawyer still passionately felt that her parents moving unfairly removed her from her peers, family, and normalcy. I don't judge her. I think her experiences are valid. Clearly, it left a lasting impact and impression on her … an impact I sincerely believe impacted her heart. Her story was a matter of her heart!

Whether you agree with the content of your lifeline or not, rest in knowing that you still have space on your lifeline. You can impact some of the remaining time with the power of reframing your life into a positive light. Taking the step toward racial reconciliation is a great addition to your lifeline. I would encourage you to mark today on your lifeline. It is significant!

6

My Story

My life is my book. My skin is my cover. Please don't judge my book by its cover.

—LaToya J. Burrell

With no doubt about it, I know what poverty looks like. When you are in poverty, you don't know it. I often hear people say, "We were poor, but we didn't know," or "We were poor, but we were happy." That's me! Despite food stamps or any other form of government assistance, I never felt impoverished. My mother was a provider. I never felt less than and never went without anything. We always had more than enough!

My parents were teenagers when I was born and were never married to one another. As a first-generation college student, I don't like the misperception that first-generation college students or those from single-parent homes cannot succeed. My mother got married when I was a teenager, and I am thankful for having love and support from both sides of my family and from my stepfather. My grandparents and aunts and uncles from both sides have always supported and loved me.

I vividly remember my first exposure to drugs. Of course, I have never used any form of drugs, but I had exposure. My first time seeing someone snort a powdered drug substance was at my junior high school bus stop. Typically, we waited in the same area for the bus as the high school students. Despite the length of the street, our bus driver did not stop in front of every home. There were a few designated stops along the street, and we were expected to walk to the nearest stop. It was not common for adults to be outside at the bus stop with teenaged students.

One morning, one of the high school boys, who I knew well, put the powder on his arm and snorted it before boarding the school bus. My heart was broken. I never told my mother. Many times, I also saw what I was pretty sure were drug deals. Despite my exposure to drugs, I entered college not knowing that marijuana and its street name, weed, were synonymous.

The famous nineties campaigns, which included "Just Say No" and Drug Abuse Resistance Education, also known as "D.A.R.E.," certainly explained to us that drugs were bad and that we should avoid them at all cost, but the campaigns used the formal names, not the street names I was exposed to. When I finally made the connection that weed was marijuana, my mind was perplexed, as I knew many people, often under the age of eighteen, who smoked marijuana.

On another occasion, at this same bus stop, one of my friends asked another girl why she was wearing a winter coat during Louisiana's September heat. She insisted that she was cold. We later found out that this junior high school-aged girl was scared and intentionally hiding her pregnancy under that jacket.

I knew many teenagers, friends, and family who ended up pregnant in their teen years. Typically, this would result in an initial upset from the parents of those teens, followed by acceptance and excitement for the arrival of the baby. This hit home for me when my younger sister was one of those pregnant teens. I blamed myself initially because as her older sister, I wish I had talked to her more about sex and life in general. I was heartbroken because I felt that she would miss out on college and knew her life would change.

The day that I found out she was pregnant, in tears, I immediately applied for my college graduation. I opted to finish college one semester early because I felt that my sister and her baby would need me. She did have a healthy baby boy who is now in high school. Despite her new baby, she graduated both high school and college, without delay. She married the father of her baby and is now a pharmacist. I know that is not how the story goes for everyone, but I am thankful that God kept her.

Reflecting on my childhood, I am reminded that our experiences are unique. Some people's only concern at the start of a school day is what to wear, while others are concerned about getting a solid breakfast, drugs, and teen pregnancy at the bus stop. This reflection demonstrates how your neighborhood and upbringing in their very nature can be indirect barriers to education, access, and success.

In college, a young black female student told me, "You cannot relate to struggle because I know you are a daddy's girl from a world unlike mine. I know your parents provide your every need." Boy, she couldn't be more wrong. I

worked hard for what I had. My first job was at the age of
fifteen as I served as the birthday girl at the local McDonald's. I was happy for my $5.15 per hour. I was making my
own money and I was proud of that.

The first time I was called the N-word was in elementary school. I didn't do anything to provoke it, and no child
deserves that kind of verbal abuse, ever. I vividly recall the
racial tension and racial divide I indirectly experienced between elementary and high school.

In 2001, my high school still had a 70/30 rule. This unwritten, but largely enforced, rule suggested that the homecoming court or cheerleading squads could only,
conveniently, be 30% black because that was the student
population. This antiquated rule dated back to before the
1980s, and a racial census was not taken annually to adjust
these numbers.

This 70/30 rule only applied to the homecoming court
and the cheerleading squad, not to the predominately black
football or basketball teams, both known for frequently receiving state recognition for its talent. In writing this book,
I inquired about whether the rule still existed. By its design,
many of my white classmates indicated that they never
knew the rule even existed and were appalled. I also received a response confirming that this rule extended beyond the school into certain recreational sports in the town.

I was voted homecoming queen in 2001, serving as one
of the three black females in the top ten that year. At the
time, I was working at McDonald's. I will never forget, a
white classmate, who was also in the top ten of the homecoming court, and her mom came to McDonald's. Her mom
in a snarky voice, said to me, "Wow, what are the odds—a
queen who works at McDonald's." This statement has

stuck with me almost twenty years later. I share this experience because it is one of the first times I experienced a blatant microaggression. Although this example was more blunt, it nonetheless was a microaggression.

For me, Claire Huxtable was my career role model. She made me feel confident that I could be a professional black woman, a mother, and a wife. *The Cosby Show* demonstrated to me that I, like Claire, could be a lawyer, I could have a husband to love me, who could also be a doctor, and we could have children and a family. Though to many *The Cosby Show* was TV, to me, it was hope. Don't get me wrong—I had a great childhood. I didn't know what I didn't know. My childhood in the 80s and 90s was before the World Wide Web, social media, and overall connectivity. Google was non-existent.

I can't say I wanted to be a lawyer as a kid. The one and only lawyer I knew personally as a kid was not a relative or even someone I had access to. Today, my children, nieces, and nephews have lawyers, doctors, and other professionals in their immediate family.

When I reflect on my formal education, my entire childhood education and collegiate education resulted in me often being one of the only black students. The word often used to describe this is tokenism. I was often that "token" black person. I have been that "black" friend before.

When I was in college, I applied to be a University Orientation leader. The application process was rigorous. I was selected and served for two years. I learned many lessons during this experience and would not change the friendships and lessons. Like many of my other experiences, only a small number of black students were selected.

During my first year, out of twenty-four students selected from the applicant pool of over two hundred, twenty were white and four were black. I did not know the other three black students, but naturally, we clung to one another. Perhaps the reason may be similar to many of the reasons outlined in Beverly Tatum's book, *Why Are All the Black Kids Sitting Together in the Cafeteria?*

As time went on, the other three black students became my great friends. Our beloved leader said she did not want us to clump together and wanted us to mingle with others who didn't look like us. "No clumping, no clumping," she would constantly say in her southern accent while chewing gum!

On this one memorable occasion, ironically, we were having lunch during our summer training retreat. The other three black students and I sat together. We were pointed out and asked to move. "No clumping, mix it up." I know that our leader had good intentions, but it wasn't fair. I quickly spoke up and said, "Why are you making us move and not the other tables?" One table was full of white girls from the same sorority. The other table was filled with white girls from a different sorority. We pointed out to her that they were also clumping. She quickly glanced at them to check and agreed. She also made them separate.

You see, her unconscious idea of clumping initially was largely based on race. When all other tables were forced to integrate with different sororities, we were then ok with not clumping together with those of the same race. Race was a difference she could not avoid seeing with her visible eye, and she tried hard to ensure that we were desegregated, but she did not pay attention to the non-visible separators until they were pointed out. I often think of this experience when

I hear people insist that they don't see color. In that moment, color was the obvious thing that caused us to stand out as a segregated table.

Although I had an amazing college experience, the reality is the university was about 65% white and 35% black. Notice I don't have an *others* percentage. I don't recall other races being represented, and if they were, it was likely less than 1% or the others self-identified with the race that closest matched their skin color.

I further remember students who I was certain had African American roots self-identify and conveniently pass as white. If you do not know what passing is, it is when a lighter or fair-skinned black person chooses to allow others to presume they are white. Many of the white people I went to school with were oblivious to passing, and even different shades. I know this may be hard to believe, but it was true.

My cousin, whose skin was nearly white, proudly identified as being African American. One day, a white friend heard her comment about wanting to pledge one of the historically black sororities. This white friend said, "That is great. You will break barriers as the first white member on campus." When my cousin declared she was in fact black, with a confused look, our white friend said, "What?" She confirmed that she honestly did not have a clue.

Race relations were common and consistent with what was expected and experienced in the south. I recall learning that a white fraternity, with a known history of racism, had a slave auction on campus. The purpose was for them to show up in blackface, dressed as slaves. Girls would buy them via auction and they would be their slaves for the day. This was a well-known fundraiser for the fraternity. The heartbreak was knowing some of the white students in that fraternity because we either worked together, took classes together, or served as orientation leaders together.

After college, I attended law school, and make no mistake about it, I enjoyed those three years. I grew academically, personally, and professionally. I had professors who cared genuinely for our well-being and success. I performed well and felt compelled to take advantage of law firm opportunities presented to me despite my interest in teaching.

Some of the racial experiences persisted as I entered law school. During orientation, the question was posed, "Why do you want to be a lawyer"? I heard many of my peers say, "I want to be a family lawyer," "I want to be a corporate lawyer," or "I want to be a civil rights advocate."

My response, which seemed out of place, was simply, "I want to be a college professor." In response, a white female professor told me that only the top 10% of law school graduates can be professors. She did not further encourage me. She just presumed I would not be in that top ten, at least that is the message she sent. I did end up being in the top 10%, but I often think about the power of words and affirmations.

Tokenism carried over into the practice of law. I was the first black female to work at one of the law firms. My boss never said it, but I would often say he isn't concerned about black and white but about green. His goal was to make money. Within two years, two other black female attorneys were hired as well.

A good friend called me and said, "I see your firm hired another black lawyer." She then jokingly said, "You must be about to be fired because you know they won't keep all of y'all at the same time, right." This very comment is something that black people frequently experience—token-ism, causing a sense of internal competition and insecurity. It is not uncommon for black employees to be resistant to embracing one another because they don't want to be viewed as clumpers ... they don't want to be viewed as loud ... they don't want to be stereotyped. They don't want the "other" black person to replace them if the business feels a need to only have one token. This is a sad reality.

I recall two events that occurred when I was practicing law. One is when a white male coworker and I were driving from Louisiana to Texas for a deposition. We elected to drive because the connecting flight proved to be an incon-venience. We were warned that our route would include passing through a known racist town in Texas. This was 2011, but we had to worry about being seen in the car as a biracial "couple." Although we were co-workers and not a couple, we didn't want to run the risk of our wedding rings being viewed as a sign that we were committed to one an-other.

Despite the warnings, we agreed that it was nonsense and that we would still drive. When we reached the town, I could sense from the look of some of the buildings and the display of confederate flags that we likely were properly informed. I told my coworker, "You know what, I will re-cline my seat, and I am asking you to drive the speed limit, drive carefully, and get us the heck out of this town."

I elected to take a flight home as opposed to driving back with my coworker. Fast-forward to June 2020 as my husband and I drove from Minnesota to Louisiana to see family. We did not want to risk flying with two small kids, amid COVID-19. Unfortunately, similar concerns reso-nated with us. My husband and I carefully plotted when we would leave and where we would stop as we embarked on this eighteen-hour drive. We felt the need to ensure that we were not forced to drive through unknown cities at night. No, we are not afraid of the dark, but we were afraid of being black, in an unknown place, in the dark.

The second occasion was when I attended a mediation with my senior partner. One of the other attorneys, from another Louisiana firm, ironically from one of the River Parishes and who I knew made a lot of money representing black people in explosion cases against large refinery plants in my hometown, first presumed I was the court reporter, then presumed I was the secretary, then a paralegal, despite previous introductions.

After my senior partner corrected him and reintroduced me as his associate attorney, he proceeded to make a tar baby joke, both offensive and completely out of context. My senior partner, a white male, said, "What did you just say?" and immediately corrected him. He then apologized to me and assured me that the man was out of line. I wanted to remind the man that his clientele was largely people who looked like me, but the quiet black girl who doesn't want to look like an angry black woman refrained from doing so. These are two small representative examples.

I moved to Minneapolis in 2013, and my early observation was how diverse the twin cities are. I do not mean just black and white, but true diversity ... Somali and many first- and second-generation African cultures, Hmong, German, Italian, Swedish, etc. It is really a melting pot. It was the first time I was challenged to pay attention to microaggressions and implicit bias (we will discuss these concepts later).

With one of my five Gallop strengths being harmony, I do not like controversy. I know, how odd, a lawyer who does not like to argue. I will argue in court any day, but in my ideal world, everything and everyone would be harmonious. I do know that's not the reality, but this is driven by my desire to lead a life of joy and harmony!

My purpose as a lifelong learner is to bring others along with me and serve as an educator. Education has catapulted me in my life, and my children are situated in a different setting than I was as a child. I may be defined as type A. I appreciate my level of organization and attentiveness, and I have learned to embrace what Gallup calls my five strengths: Achiever, Learner, Focus, Discipline, and Harmony.

Overall, in reflecting on my life, there are many occurrences that many would place on the right side of their lifeline. I choose to see the value in these experiences and lessons. I encourage you to see the value and power in reframing adverse experiences in your life. I also share these experiences, in a vulnerable sense, to let you see that my life has not been perfect and I have had my fair share of racial occurrences—some subtle and others more in your face. Now that we have done the introductions, it is time to go deeper! The path to racial reconciliation and healing is a marathon, not a sprint! Are you ready to continue this journey?

7

Educate and Humble Yourself:
Learn and Listen

Wisdom is not like money, to be tied up and hidden.

—Akan proverb

This next section of this book will explore educating and humbling yourself (listening and learning). It is divided into three main sections: A Brief History Lesson (listening and learning), The Different Stages (learning), and The Questions (listening and learning). The history lesson will briefly explore American history with a focus on the African American experience, beginning with 1619 to the present day. When reviewing the history, I encourage you to digest the content, ask questions, discuss with your Growth Group, and do outside research, including watching documentaries and movies, reading other sources, and listening to podcasts and TED Talks.

The Different Stages section will explore different stages often experienced when taking the journey toward racial reconciliation. The Top Ten Questions are a series of questions frequently raised when exploring racism or racial reconciliation. I encourage you to do these questions in multiple sessions with your Growth Group. This is a cyclical process, not a strict four-step process. Despite where you begin in this cycle, my end goal is for you to Be Bold! Simply embarking on this journey may have taken boldness ... thus for you, being bold may be your first step. The process may look like this:

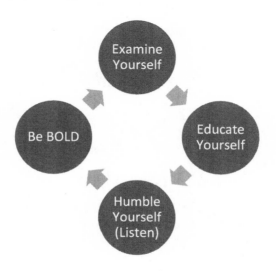

Notice the cyclical depiction does not suggest where you should start, nor does it suggest an end. This cyclical process, for many, will be ongoing. Where you start is not as important as what you gain from this process! In the previous chapters, we discussed "Examine Yourself." In the next chapters, we will cover "Educate Yourself" and "Humble Yourself." Are you ready to humble yourself, listen, and learn?

8

A Brief History Lesson

History repeats itself endlessly for those who are un-willing to learn from the past.

—Leon Brown

In the wake of the death of George Floyd, America is listening … America is watching … America is reading … America is talking! Social media and the news began to be flooded with new information about history that, unfortunately, was either intentionally suppressed or we just did not learn about it.

To understand systematic oppression, we must know the history of America. Not just some of the history, but the truth, the whole truth, and nothing but the truth. This includes from 1619, when the first documented slaves were taken from Africa and brought to America, to when some slaves were set "free" to 1863, when the Emancipation Proclamation was signed. This includes the Thirteenth Amendment, which declared that all slaves were free in January 1865 to June 1865, when other slaves finally received word that they were free. Now this information alone represents an entire course in itself, but I will briefly summarize these significant events.

Often, race-related discussions make the faulty presumptions that everyone has the same foundational knowledge about history. This presumption is dangerous and misplaced, as many of us were not taught basics about black history as it is engrained in overall American history.

Most people know the basics ... Martin Luther King Jr., Rosa Parks, Harriet Tubman, Fredrick Douglass, and the word slavery, but that often doesn't include any depth or even a taste of the tip of the iceberg.

Harriet Washington, author of *Medical Apartheid,* said, "Trying to understand a historical problem without knowing its history is like trying to treat a patient without eliciting a thorough medical history ... you are doomed to failure."[7] We want to understand the historical problems created as a result of slavery and racism. As such, it is imperative to have a brief history lesson. The goal is for this historical foundation to frame some of the very thoughts and issues experienced today.

Taken from Africa

History books suggest that slavery began in 1619, documenting August as the month that a boat of Africans, who were taken captive and brought to America, arrived in Jamestown, Virginia. Those referred to as slaves were not brought to America to enjoy the land of the free and the home of the brave. Some historians suggest that the first slaves were brought to America as early as 1400. Others suggest that we do not know if they were stolen, sold, or came voluntarily.

A Brief History Lesson

Other stories suggest that Christopher Columbus brought slaves to America before 1619. I don't know about you, but my history memory of Christopher Columbus is all about a heroic man, 1492, and the Nina, Pinta, and Santa Maria. I was tested on memorizing that information and don't recall any discussion about slaves. In fact, I don't remember much discussion at all about slavery in my formal education. My education about slavery began with the inadvertent watching of the movie *Roots*.

One thing not for debate is regardless of when they came or how they got to America, the result was slavery and oppression.

Although we may never agree on the true arrival date, we should be able to agree on two things: First, slavery took place in America for almost 250 years, and second, the very act of slavery was inhumane and *wrong*! Some history talks about the route from Africa and conditions on slave boats.

Experts say that sharks still swarm the Atlantic slave trade route because of the heavy human remains found along the route from enslaved African's either being thrown aboard or choosing to jump to their deaths. Now, if we want to educate ourselves on the unfortunate history of slavery, there is no shortage of books, documentaries, movies, websites, scholarly articles, symposiums, and journals. We don't have to search far.

I am from southern Louisiana, and plantation tours are common. I have a confession. I grew up a few miles away from a plantation known for tours. It wasn't until 2015 when one of my good Minnesota native friends took her first trip to Louisiana with me and specifically requested to do a plantation tour. I obliged and we visited the Whitney Plantation.

Deep down inside, I didn't want to go ... after all, I grew up miles away and never felt the need to go. She initially said she wanted to go on a swamp tour and plantation tour, but due to time restraints, we only had time for one. I am deathly afraid of alligators, but a part of me felt like visiting a plantation and facing the truth was scarier than seeing an alligator. As a gracious hostess, I allowed her to choose, and she elected to visit the plantation. The tour was heartbreaking, yet eye-opening, and I am grateful that my friend chose the plantation tour.

The tour guide was full of knowledge and life, and, ironically, I, my friend, and our husbands were the only black people on the tour. The tour guide also presumed that we were tourists. With embarrassment, I told her that I actually grew up locally.

She then asked, "Who are your people?"

"My mother's maiden name is Darensbourg," I said.

"Yes, that's German," she immediately replied.

I hunched my shoulders and nodded my head, suggesting that I already knew and was agreeing with her. I was too embarrassed to say, "I don't know."

She replied, "Yes, baby" with her Southern accent and proceeded to give me a brief history lesson on why German men came to America and the role they ultimately played in teaching slaves how to cultivate the land.

Apparently, the marshland is similar. Why was this my first-time hearing this? Why did I not know German history? Since then, I have learned that Germans were said to be industrious farmers who saved New Orleans from famine. This reminds me that slavery robbed African Americans of knowing our true origins. I wish I knew the exact

African region. Am I Liberian or Nigerian? It is heartbreaking not to know this information with certainty.

The plantation tour also broke my heart to look at a large map depicting the River Road, which runs through the River Parishes in Louisiana, a few miles south of New Orleans. Viewing these maps was the unfortunate reminder that the plantations still carry the slave owner's names to this day. Many subdivisions carry the plantation's name as the entire subdivision name. I knew the areas on the map all too well. I can view this in two ways: 1. The unfortunate fact that the plantation still carries its name or 2. The fact that African Americans can now purchase and own land on these plantations. Either way, it is truth.

Partially Free

For almost 250 years, slavery was commonplace in America. Simple math suggests that generations are counted in about twenty-year increments. With that math and almost 250 years of slavery, we are talking about approximately twelve generations of slavery. To add insult to injury, at this time, slavery was justified because we were not viewed as human.

In 1787, the Three-Fifths Compromise was birthed.[8] This compromise was reached at the Constitutional Convention as a compromise to determine the best way to count slaves in state populations for legislative representation purposes (ultimately to benefit the master, not the slave). The conclusion was for only three of every five slaves to count. So did that mean only 3/5 of each black person mattered or that we would just presume that two out of every five black people did not matter? Regardless, we know, based on things like this compromise, slavery was intentional and used to economically provide wealth for the master.

For almost 250 years, people known as slaves were brutally treated, subjected to harsh living conditions, and were forced to provide free labor. Slaves were not allowed to learn to read or write, they were not allowed to marry, and often the family unit was non-existent. The babies of female slaves were often taken from them at birth and sold. Male slaves were demasculinized as they were beaten, raped, and tortured in front of others. Rape was common, and the conditions were unconscionable.

In 1857, the Supreme Court decision in *Dred Scott v. Sandford*[9] determined that slaves were property and thus had no rights. Therefore, they didn't have the right to sue or have other constitutionally guaranteed rights. After over 250 years of inhumane treatment, the formal system of slavery eventually came to an end.

Abraham Lincoln and The Emancipation Proclamation are well-known and taught in American history and notated as the end of slavery. I encourage every reader to read the actual content of the Emancipation Proclamation, which is only 719 words in its entirety. The Proclamation took effect on January 1, 1863.

As we learn about Abraham Lincoln and the Emancipation Proclamation, we are also taught about the Civil War, which spanned from 1861–1865. This is an important historical context for both the signing and scope of the proclamation. Many people believe that the proclamation freed all slaves, but unfortunately, it did not. Here is an excerpt (317 of the 719 words):

Now, therefore I, Abraham Lincoln, President of the United States, by virtue of the power in me vested as Commander-in-Chief, of the Army and Navy of the United States in time of actual armed rebellion against the authority and government of the United States, and as a fit and necessary war measure for suppressing said rebellion, do, on this first day of January, in the year of our Lord one thousand eight hundred and sixty-three, and in accordance with my purpose so to do publicly proclaimed for the full period of one hundred days, from the day first above mentioned, order and designate as the States and parts of States wherein the people thereof respectively, *are this day in rebellion against the United States*, the following, to wit: Arkansas, Texas, Louisiana, *(except the Parishes of St. Bernard, Plaquemines, Jefferson, St. John, St. Charles, St. James Ascension, Assumption, Terrebonne, Lafourche, St. Mary, St. Martin, and Orleans, including the City of New Orleans)* Mississippi, Alabama, Florida, Georgia, South Carolina, North Carolina, and Virginia, (except the forty-eight counties designated as West Virginia, and also the counties of Berkley, Accomack, Northampton, Elizabeth City, York, Princess Ann, and Norfolk, including the cities of Norfolk and Portsmouth[)], and which excepted parts, are for the present, left precisely as if this proclamation were not issued.

And by virtue of the power, and for the purpose aforesaid, I do order and declare that all persons held as slaves within said designated States, and parts of States, are, and henceforward shall be free; and that the Executive government of the United States, including the military and naval authorities thereof, will recognize and maintain the freedom of said persons.

And I hereby enjoin upon the people so declared to be free to abstain from all violence, unless in necessary self-defen[s]e; and I recommend to them that, in all cases when allowed, they labor faithfully for reasonable wages. (Abraham Lincoln, Emancipation Proclamation, emphasis added)

While the proclamation certainly declared some slaves to be free, note the italicized exceptions. This is pivotal to me, as I am from St. Charles Parish. Also, note that the designated areas were *in rebellion against the United States,* which requires a history lesson within itself. Despite the proclamation, all slaves were not free. This is not the version commonly taught in constitutional or historical studies.

The Thirteenth Amendment

The Thirteenth Amendment of the Constitution states:

Neither slavery nor involuntary servitude, except as a punishment for crime whereof the party shall have been duly convicted, shall exist within the United States, or any place subject to their jurisdiction.

Notice the date and exception in the Thirteenth Amendment. It was passed by Congress on January 31, 1865. The exception to the new Amendment clearly states that slavery or involuntary servitude is acceptable as a punishment for a crime, if "duly convicted." I will not further expound on the Thirteenth Amendment, but I wish to make two final points:

1. This is two years after the Emancipation Proclamation. As such, there are no longer exceptions for slaves located in certain geographic limitations, as listed in the 1863 proclamation, and enslavement is no longer allowed against anyone who is a free, "non-convicted criminal."
2. Formal education historically teaches about the Bill of Rights only, which does not include the Thirteenth Amendment.

Constitutional Law is complex. I encourage every reader to watch the documentary *13th* by Ava DuVernay.[10] This 2016 documentary focuses on systemic racism, both historically and present day, in the United States criminal justice system. Ava DuVernay explores mass incarceration and how the exception in the Thirteenth Amendment is viewed as a loophole to the actual ending of slavery. The documentary suggests that slavery has not ended but has essentially been altered and often plays out in the criminal justice and prison system.

In addition to studying the Thirteenth Amendment, I encourage you to do a brief study on the Civil War and its relationship to the Thirteenth Amendment. Further, in the context of the Emancipation Proclamation and the Thirteenth Amendment, it is worth noting that Abraham Lincoln was the president during both years. He was the sixteenth President of the United States and was the first assassinated US president (1861–1865).

Some other interesting history is that Abraham Lincoln was the first presidential face to be minted to a US coin. His face was added to the penny in 1909 and remains to this day. The current nickel includes the face of Thomas Jefferson, the current dime includes the face of Franklin Roosevelt, and the current quarter includes the face of George Washington. There is a lot of history and differing context on what exactly was on the back of coins and when the coins entered circulation, but Lincoln was the first to be placed on the front.

Here is a visual depiction of the U.S coins:

Some say the color and direction is no coincidence. I was taught as a young girl that racial symbolism was embedded in the very coins that still circulate today as US currency. Apparently, the message sent from the money was that other leaders felt that he, Abraham Lincoln, turned his back on them to free brown slaves.

Other versions suggest that the direction is a mere co-incidence based on the direction of his portrait. This does not suggest that Lincoln's actions do not in themselves warrant further exploration, but for the sake of this brief history lesson, I will not expound on his life.

Now, I cannot deny that the penny is brown, it has the least value of all coins, and it is the only coin where the presidential face is looking to the right. After doing some research, my final thought is whether a coincidence or not, instead of digging for truth, I am more bothered by the why. Why is America's history so rooted in racism that I would not be surprised if the color, value, and directions were intentional and not a mere coincidence?

Juneteenth

Despite the Thirteenth Amendment, we must be reminded that in 1865, news did not travel at the same speed as it does in 2020. For approximately two-and-a-half years, some slaves were unaware that per the newly signed Amendment, they were free. On June 19, 1865, the final group of southern slaves learned of their freedom. This required federal troops to take control of the state of Texas to ensure that all enslaved people were free. Now we are not talking about one or two slaves. History documents the group of unaware slaves to be nearly 250,000 in number.

Juneteenth is celebrated to mark the official end of formal slavery. I was taught that the name Juneteenth was derived from knowing that the freedom was discovered in June, but that the exact day was unknown. However, it was narrowed to between the thirteenth through nineteenth of June, hence Juneteenth. As of June 2020, forty-seven states recognized Juneteenth as a full or partial holiday (all, except Hawaii and North and South Dakota).[11] Most states recognized Juneteenth between 2000–2019, with a few state recognitions dating back to the 1980s (Texas only) and 1990s (Minnesota, Florida, and Oklahoma only). The first documented state and date was Texas in 1980. Every June, many celebrations take place in African American communities across the country to celebrate Juneteenth.

Now here we are in 2020, and as I write this page on June 12, 2020, Juneteenth is trending on social media. Why? Not because it's less than a week away but because it has been given attention due to recent announcements from the White House. With 2020 as an election year, Donald Trump announced that he would host his first rally in months on June 19, 2020 in Tulsa, Oklahoma. Why is this a big deal? Does it matter? Should it matter? Is it a coincidence? Is it insensitive? Let me give some context. You just read about Juneteenth, but take a second and refill your coffee cup, so I can tell you about Tulsa, Oklahoma.

Tulsa, Oklahoma

After formal and legal slavery officially ended, African Americans began to build communities across the United States. Tulsa, Oklahoma is known for the historic Black Wall Street and business acumen. In summary, Black Wall Street began in 1906 when the first black business was opened, specifically in what became known as the Greenwood community of Tulsa.

The first businessman was said to have the vision of creating something for black people by black people. The self-sufficient community filled with black-owned businesses flourished until it was burned to the ground in 1921. Black Wall Street encompassed one of the most prosperous African American communities at the time.

This topic is worth researching, and I appreciate the fact that Donald Trump announced that he would have a rally in Tulsa on Juneteenth in 2020. Although his administration suggested that it was a coincidence and not designed to be disrespectful, fact-checkers suggested that Tulsa, Oklahoma is not a place where he is lacking in votes or supporters.

While the result was the decision to cancel the rally, the outcome was many Americans, white and black, questioning what is the big deal with Tulsa and June 19th? Both questions caused people to research Tulsa and Juneteenth, and as a result, many also learned about Black Wall Street.

The Tulsa, Oklahoma massacre took place on Memorial Day weekend in 1921 when mobs of white men attacked black businesses and residents. The targeted area was said to be Black Wall Street. Like many other times in American history, where allegedly a black male assaulted a white woman, the alleged cause for the mob's presence was to find and lynch the black male being accused. The result was the burning of thirty-five city blocks, which included African American businesses and communities, seen as a threat because of their wealth and viability.

Some called the event a race riot, but as many African Americans were slaughtered, others have suggested that a more fitting descriptor of this event is a massacre. It is said that after the massacre, many survivors fled the city, and those who remained were silent.

It was not until 1996 that the massacre was studied, seventy-five years later. More disturbingly, the massacre has not been taught in Oklahoma schools as a part of the history curriculum. It was announced in February 2020 that nearly one hundred years later, the topic will finally become a part of the curriculum for the Oklahoma schools.[12] An HBO series, *Watchmen*, also brings attention to the Tulsa Massacre.[13] The nine-show series aired in the Fall of 2019, and the opening episode setting depicted the Tulsa Massacre.

COVID-19 allowed me to have additional time. I found myself having sleepless nights reading, watching, and just overall expanding my mind. Documentary after documentary, I realized there was so much history that I have never been taught. Further, I reminded myself of the many movies designed to share the history of slavery in America and how those movies typically felt more like a nightmare to me and left me enraged. I often avoided movies that reminded me of the brutal enslavement my people endured for over 250 years.

I immediately found myself rewatching movies and documentaries, such as *Rosewood* and *Selma,* and forcing myself to watch some movies for the first time like *Twelve Years a Slave*. Unfortunately, Tulsa is not the only massacre in America, post-slavery. A few other documented massacres, with the target being African Americans, took place in many other places, including the following:

- Colfax, Louisiana 1873
- Wilmington, North Carolina 1898
- Atlanta, Georgia 1906
- Elaine, Arkansas 1919
- Rosewood, Florida 1923

These massacres were outlined in a Black Entertainment Television (BET) news article[14], published in June 2020. This article briefly discussed the above listed massacres and included videos explaining each. I urge you to take some time to educate yourself about these massacres. One common trend across these historical documentaries include black people attempting to pursue life, wealth, success, and autonomy. Another common trend was non-violent, self-contained, and self-sufficient African Americans. Learn about these other massacres. Knowledge is power.

Black Codes, Jim Crow, and the Civil Rights Act of 1964

Post-slavery, former slaves, now "free," worked hard to create economic stability and freedom during the period known as Reconstruction. When set free, they walked away from plantations with nothing—no land, no money, nothing except hope for a brighter tomorrow.

The first black codes were created in southern states in 1865 and 1866 and remained in effect until Reconstruction began in 1866. The purpose of the black codes was to control, and ultimately limit, the freedoms of African Americans recently declared free. It is said the black codes had its "roots in the slave codes," previously used to govern slaves, and was designed to maintain white supremacy.[15]

The black codes caused African Americans to continue to serve as cheap labor and were enforced by newly created police forces, which were all white.[16] Black codes were created by states, and as such, content varied across states. Here are a few examples of restrictions placed on black codes from various states:

- Permission to travel
- Segregation
- Laws and punishments
- Limited choice in employment and strict labor contracts
- Permission required from employers to sell farm produce
- Banned from bearing arms
- Orphans placed into forced apprenticeships with previous slave-owners
- Prevention of Freedmen from voting or serving on juries

As a Louisiana native, one example of a black code that hit home was learning of the purpose of the *fleur de lis* symbol, as used during slavery. This symbol is associated with the New Orleans Saints football team and is also personally used as interior décor in my home. We see it as a symbol of our Louisiana roots, or so I thought.

I was saddened to learn that during the black code era, Louisiana's black codes were outlined in the Code Noir.[17] Within the context, the *fleur de lis* was branded on slaves as a form of punishment for being in violation of one of the black codes or running away. The more we know!

Jim Crow Laws and the Civil Rights Act of 1964

Once Reconstruction ended, many black codes were reenacted or redesigned in the form of Jim Crow laws, beginning in 1877. They were designed to enforce and promote racial segregation heavily in Southern Confederate states. Jim Crow laws were largely created in the 1870s and 1880s and enforced until 1965.

Despite challenges, a landmark Supreme Court decision, *Plessy v. Ferguson*, upheld Jim Crow laws, with the now well-known "separate but equal doctrine."[18] The problem with this doctrine, beyond the obvious moral issues attempting to justify separate, is that the "but equal" portion was not effectively practiced. Although the *Plessy* case related to public transportation, the impact was extended to buses, facilities, restaurants, schools, and other public facilities.

Another landmark Supreme Court case was the 1954 *Brown v. Board of Education*[19] case, which held that racial segregation in public schools was not constitutional. In this case, the main argument made was that schools for black children were not equal. Other major events took place post the *Brown* case, including Rosa Parks and her refusal to move, the Montgomery Bus Boycott, and other significant events during the Civil Rights movement. The *Brown* case ultimately led to the overturning of laws that allowed segregation in public places.

Ultimately, the Civil Rights Act of 1964 was passed and overturned the decision of *Plessy v. Ferguson*. Specifically, the Act determined that all persons are entitled to the same treatment, without "discrimination or segregation on the ground of race, color, religion, or national origin." Since then, there have been other Supreme Court cases to define these pivotal terms and to ensure proper enforcement.

Other History: 1865–present

How does one even begin to write about 155 years of history? The act alone should be a compilation of books, not a few pages in this book. I urge you not to stop here in educating yourself about history. My goal is to provide a very limited summary of the history in post-slavery America. To avoid reinventing the wheel, I have included a timeline below, which outlines black history from 1865–2006.[20]

1865

- The Civil War ends; the Thirteenth Amendment, abolishing slavery, is ratified.

1868

- The Fourteenth Amendment, which requires equal protection under the law to all persons, is ratified.

1870

- The Fifteenth Amendment, which bans racial discrimination in voting, is ratified.

1896

- The Supreme Court approves the "separate but equal" segregation doctrine.

1909

- The National Negro Committee convenes. This leads to the founding of the National Association for the Advancement of Colored People (NAACP).

1925

- In its first national demonstration, the Ku Klux Klan marches on Washington, DC.

1948

- President Truman issues an executive order outlawing segregation in the US military.

1954

- The Supreme Court declares school segregation unconstitutional in its ruling on *Brown v. Board of Education* of Topeka, Kansas.

1955

- Rosa Parks is jailed for refusing to move to the back of a Montgomery, Alabama, bus. A boycott follows, and the bus segregation ordinance is declared unconstitutional.

- The Federal Interstate Commerce Commission bans segregation on interstate trains and buses.

1957

- Arkansas Governor Orval Faubus uses the National Guard to block nine black students from attending Little Rock High School. Following a court order, President Eisenhower sends in federal troops to allow the black students to enter the school.

1960

- Four black college students begin sit-ins at the lunch counter of a Greensboro, North Carolina restaurant, where black patrons are not served.

1961

- Freedom Rides begin from Washington, DC, into Southern states. Student volunteers are bused in to test new laws prohibiting segregation.

1962

- President Kennedy sends federal troops to the University of Mississippi to end riots so that James Meredith, the school's first black student, can attend.

- The Supreme Court rules that segregation is unconstitutional in all transportation facilities.
- The Department of Defense orders complete integration of military reserve units, excluding the National Guard.

1963

- Civil rights leader Medgar Evers is killed by a sniper's bullet.
- Dr. Martin Luther King Jr. delivers his "I Have a Dream" speech to hundreds of thousands at the March on Washington, DC.
- A church bombing in Birmingham, Alabama leaves four young black girls dead.

1964

- Congress passes the Civil Rights Act, declaring discrimination based on race illegal.
- The Twenty-Fourth Amendment abolishes the poll tax, which originally had been established in the South after Reconstruction to make it difficult for poor blacks to vote.
- Three civil rights workers, two white and one black man, disappear in Mississippi. They were found buried six weeks later.

1965

- A march from Selma to Montgomery, Alabama is organized to demand protection for voting rights.
- Malcolm X, a longtime minister of the Nation of Islam, is assassinated. He had rejected Dr. Martin Luther King, Jr.'s policies of non-violence and preached black pride and economic self-reliance for blacks. He eventually became a Muslim and broke with Nation of Islam leader Elijah Muhammad.
- A new Voting Rights Act, which made it illegal to force would-be voters to pass literacy tests in order to vote, is signed.

1967

- Thurgood Marshall becomes the first black to be named to the Supreme Court.

1968

- Dr. Martin Luther King Jr. is assassinated in Memphis, Tennessee. James Earl Ray pleaded guilty of the crime in March 1969 and was sentenced to ninety-nine years in prison.
- President Lyndon B. Johnson signs the Civil Rights Act of 1968, which prohibits discrimination in the sale, rental, and financing of housing.

1976

- Negro History Week becomes Black History Month.

1978

- The Supreme Court rules, in a well-known reverse discrimination case (*Bakke*), that medical school admission programs that allow for positions based on race are unconstitutional.

1983

- The Dr. Martin Luther King Jr. federal holiday is established.

1988

- The Democratically controlled Congress overrides a presidential veto to pass the Civil Rights Restoration Act. President Ronald Reagan vetoed the law, saying it gave the federal government overreaching powers.

1990

- President George H.W. Bush vetoes a civil rights bill that he says would impose quotas for employers. A civil rights bill without quotas passes in 1991.

1995

- The Supreme Court rules that federal programs that consider race as a category for hiring must have "compelling government interest" to do so.
- The Supreme Court rules that the consideration of race in creating congressional districts is unconstitutional.

2003

- The Supreme Court upholds the University of Michigan Law School's policy, ruling that race can be one of many factors considered by colleges when selecting their students.

2005

- Edgar Ray Killen, the leader of the Mississippi murders (1964), is convicted of manslaughter on the 41st anniversary of the crimes.
- Rosa Parks dies at the age of 92.

2006

- Coretta Scott King, widow of slain civil rights leader Dr. Martin Luther King Jr., dies at the age of 78 of a stroke. Mrs. King had moved into the forefront of the civil rights movement after the passing of her husband in 1968.

A Brief History Lesson

Now, this timeline is not even a mere fraction of the story. I do not have enough space on this page to add the necessary number of zeros to represent the proper small percentage of knowledge this timeline represents. *Do not* mistake this visual depiction as the necessary history lesson. Some very basic topics I discussed in this chapter are not all included in the timeline. Also, other significant history not included is the Tuskegee Experiment that took place between 1932 and 1972.

I challenge you to not only read the timeline but further expound on this history and other history not included on the timeline. To understand history and ensure it is not repeated, we must know history. In order to grow, we must know! This knowledge is not only for white Americans but for all Americans ... for all people who want to truly understand.

As we know, in school settings, HIS-story is often taught, and unfortunately, those books either don't completely depict the inclusion of slaves, black people, and minorities. So my charge to everyone is to educate yourself about all history. I would be remiss if I didn't add to the history timeline, post-2006. Here are additions:

2008

- Barack Obama is elected 44th President of the United States.

2010

- The Fair Sentencing Act reduces sentencing disparities between crack and powder cocaine.

2011

- The MLK Memorial on the National Mall site opens.

2012

- Trayvon Martin is killed.

2013

- The Black Lives Matter movement begins, following the death of Trayvon Martin.

2015

- The Charleston Church Shooting takes place, where American white supremacists mass murdered nine African Americans during their Bible study at Emanuel African Methodist Episcopal Church.

2020

- George Floyd is killed and national protest sparks, elevating the discussion about race and racism.

Many other significant events have not been included in the initial timeline and post-2006 additions. We are in such a good place because we have easy access to information—the internet, ebooks, just an overall wealth of information. If you don't believe yourself to be a reader, that's ok. There are so many audiobooks, free lectures on YouTube, movies, documentaries, and many resources we can use to educate ourselves. So if you want to change, you must be ready to do the work necessary to learn.

It is hard to believe that in 2020 we are seeing a repeat of the civil rights movement from the 1960s. Some differences are the demographics of those protesting, the access to information, and the ability to easily share in real time, in color, what is happening. You don't have to wait to see it in black and white on the news, filtered, from the lens of the usually non-minority reporter. You can see it in color ... in real time, from multiple vantage points, different news sources, and directly on social media. We can share, comment, and filter through what we are witnessing. This allows people to be loud, and some will share who often would not have a voice, both good and bad.

As we continue to write history, my prayer is that black history will reflect changes that allow black people and other minorities to truly be seen as equals and be treated accordingly. We must understand that even in 2020, anyone of African descent, anyone of color, is still searching for freedom. 400 years later, we remain oppressed. 400 years later, we are not completely free. This short chapter is a small fraction of American history and is designed only to give context for the remainder of this book.

One final charge I give you (and also give myself) is to have a discussion with and listen and learn from someone who lived during or before the civil rights movement. A fun fact about me is that I had the privilege of meeting all eight of my great-grandparents, the first of whom did not die until I was a teenager. I also met and spent a lot of quality time with all four of my grandparents. My grandfathers, who were both father figures in my life, died in my adult years. Both of my grandmothers are still alive, and I thank God for them daily.

I challenge myself to, in the coming days, have discussions with both grandmothers, Elaine and Ella Mae, about their racial experiences throughout their lives. I also plan to talk to my eighty-year-old father-in-law, Herbert Sr. I have heard his stories of being raised in New Orleans in the 1940s and 1950s, including having to sit on the back row of the Catholic Church and tap dancing for income in the French Quarters.

I will take advantage of the history present in my immediate family. I have also heard my grandmother stress the importance of knowing history to ensure its preservation. I challenge you to do the same. After all, the more we know, the more we can grow! I will end this chapter and charge with a 1968 quote from Dr. Martin Luther King Jr.[21], which I believe is still resoundingly applicable today:

> I want to discuss the race problem tonight and I want to discuss it very honestly. I still believe that freedom is the bonus you receive for telling the truth. Ye shall know the truth and the truth shall set you free. And I do not see how we will ever solve the turbulent problem of race confronting our nation until there is an honest confrontation with it and a willing search for the

truth and a willingness to admit the truth when we discover it.

9

Different Stages

Brokenness is for a season, but lessons from it are for a lifetime.

—Priscilla Shirer

**History is not our fault. This process is not about placing blame or finding fault, but it's about finding a solution. It is not our fault ... the past, bondage, privileges, opportunities, or the lack thereof. However, it's our job to dismantle systems that persist as a result of the very history we do not want to be blamed for. It is not our fault, but it is our duty to educate ourselves and grow toward equality and justice for all.

When we become aware, we inherit an obligation to no longer be silent or idle. Once we become aware, our continued silence infers that we are complicit with the current systems. At the place of complicity, we then become susceptible to blame. Finally, although listening is required, action is also required. Your time, your energy, your voice, your platform, and your intentional support are all critical.

In this journey, there are different stages—fear zone, learning zone, and growth zone.[22] In the fear zone, you typically deny racism and avoid discussions about racism. The second zone is the learning zone. In this zone, ideally, you acknowledge that racism is a problem, educate yourself about racism and its impact, and listen to different perspectives. The final zone is the growth zone. In this zone, you speak out when you see racism and advocate for equality. The growth zone requires you to truly step out of the comfort zone and into a growth zone. This takes courage. This takes a commitment. This takes boldness.

Your mindset must shift to make you willing to be vulnerable. In the fear zone, you are not vulnerable. You sit in fear and comfort and lean on the excuse of not knowing what to do or say to keep from growing. Others in this group may desire more but may feel that the issues are larger than what they can contribute. I encourage you to reject these thoughts and adopt a mindset of one in the growth zone.

In the growth zone, you acknowledge that you are not perfect but that you want to grow. You continue to engage by listening and learning. You understand that you are human and that growth is often uncomfortable. Despite the discomfort, you are willing and ready to commit to growth.

If you have ever attended a diversity or race-related training, it is undeniable that at some point, if not for most of the discussion, there is a spirit of discomfort in the room. The topics in themselves cause discomfort. Hearing terms like racist, slavery, white privilege, prejudices, and whiteness cause people to visibly become flustered or uneasy about the discussions to come.

No one wants to be uncomfortable. Reading this chapter may make you uneasy. Unfortunately, change is not always comfortable and though not comfortable, topics about race are necessary. One way to overcome the discomfort is to acknowledge the discomfort and boldly declare that the discomfort will not win. Take your power back and declare that the discomfort will not dominate your mind, will not dominate the room, and will not take up any more space than necessary. In the growth zone, change happens!

10

The Top Ten Questions

To be anti-racist is a radical choice in the face of history, requiring a radical reorientation of our consciousness.

—Ibram Kendi

This section focuses on The Top Ten Questions commonly asked, in addition to the What Can I Do question. In learning and listening, we will engage by addressing these Top Ten Questions one question at a time. After each question, I will provide a brief response to the answer. The responses are not meant to be exhaustive but are designed to be starting points for dialogue.

There are suggested dialogue questions at the end of each chapter, which correspond to a question. Please use these dialogue questions to further engage with your Growth Group. Some of these discussions may be uncomfortable, but sometimes change and growth are uncomfortable.

To my white readers, these are questions you may have asked or may have wondered about. Please explore these questions with an open heart and open mind. Please be honest with your feelings and thoughts. Be ready to engage with follow-up questions and feedback about each question.

To my black readers, many black people say we do not want to watch the history because it makes us mad. It feels more like a horror movie to us. But we also must educate ourselves. Engage with these questions and listen to the perspective of others. Do not be offended by follow-up questions. Be vulnerable in sharing experiences and approach this section with an open heart and open mind.

To my non-white or black readers, you too can educate yourself on these topics and discover some biases and solutions. Racism is not a white man issue. Many of these issues are applicable to all minorities or, in general, to anyone who may have experienced bias. I welcome you to approach these questions with an open heart and mind and be sure to make it applicable to your own experiences.

To all of my readers, I encourage you not to just take my word or response to these questions but discuss the questions with your Growth Groups (listen). Do your own research (learn). Pray and examine your heart on these topics. Be bold in your discussions and share the information. At the end of this journey, boldly speak up when others pose these questions, often in a negative or uninformed way. Be the change that you want to see.

Here is a road map of the questions we will explore:

The Top Ten Questions:

1. I didn't own slaves, so why should this matter to me? I wasn't a slave, so this doesn't apply to me, does it?
2. I don't see color, so why does this apply to me?
3. I'm not racist, and when examining my heart, it's clean. I love everyone with the same love of Christ, so how does this apply to me?
4. Why do Diversity and Inclusion initiatives, and race discussions in general, focus on black and white when there are many other races, cultures, and minority groups?
5. All Lives Matter, so why do we say Black Lives Matter?
6. If black people don't commit crimes, they will not have this issue, right?
7. Why can't black people simply work harder? After all, we all have access to the same freedoms here in America, right?
8. We had a black president, and black people have good jobs and equal access. Doesn't that make everyone equal and America post-racial?
9. Why can't I just ignore racism? I am not racist, and the topic makes me uncomfortable.
10. Why protest? It doesn't work. Surely there is a more peaceful way to address these issues.

Question #1: I didn't own slaves, so why should this matter to me? I wasn't a slave, so why does this apply to me?

Of course you did not own slaves! This may be true, but we cannot deny history. But for the changes in history, would you own a slave? By your very birthright, would you have been born into the home of a slave owner and set to inherit slaves? If you are black, would you have controlled being born into slavery? I can simply argue that I am not a slave, and I am *not*! But that does not change the fact that many of my ancestors were. It does not change the fact that as I live my life, I still feel the effects of slavery since I live in America, a place that continues to have systematic oppression intertwined into the very fabric of life.

Black people who say we are not our ancestors, I agree! We are not slaves. I am not my ancestors because as Maya Angelou so eloquently stated, "I am their wildest dream."[23] I believe that slaves dreamed of being free, and we are seemingly living in that time. In respecting my roots, I must know my history. In understanding history, we must acknowledge the past. Discussing history in no way is a finger pointing or blame game.

In 2020, no one should be implicated by the past actions of others. However, if we are not willing to acknowledge the direct impact of slavery and how it indirectly impacts our lives, we are in denial. If we continue not to address history and allow the indirect implications and effects to persist, we will not successfully move forward. Slavery is America's original sin. As a country, we must repent.

As a mother, I could not imagine having a child only to have that child snatched from me to be sold to another slave master. Yes, this was the unfortunate reality. I think about the movie *Beloved*,[24] which I watched as a kid. I didn't quite grasp the magnitude then, but as a mother, I now understand that the mother in the movie preferred to kill her baby and have the baby go to the Lord as opposed to having her baby be subjected to slavery. That mother was willing to sacrifice her own safety to save her child.

Although we are not our ancestors, either black or white, we must understand history to ensure it doesn't repeat. We must acknowledge history to ensure context is given to the very real and lasting impact slavery left on us.

You see, we are not born racist; we are instead taught to hate and to be prejudicial even if indirectly taught. So in its very existence, racism relates to slavery. To heal racial tension and ultimately get to racial reconciliation, we must be willing to listen and learn … even though we did not own slaves and even though we were not slaves.

We cannot deny that systemic oppression, rooted in the history of race relations in America, causes many of us to feel the remnants of what America as a country was during the 1800s and 1900s. One example of a racial disparity and historical impact stemming from slavery is the seemingly simple nature of homeownership and overall generational wealth.

One common form of generational wealth is owning and investing in real estate. From 1619–1865, slaves were not free, let alone allowed to own property. Post-slavery, despite efforts to provide land to African Americans via the Freedman's Bureau and the promised forty acres and a mule, many now free, former slaves and their descendants had a barrier to obtaining land and homeownership. This barrier was the lack of documents required to prove their identity to gain ownership. Others who did get land died without wills, and the property often reverted to the state.

Now the broader history of African Americans and homeownership even post-slavery warrants further study. Redlining, restrictive covenants, and other mechanisms were in place to limit black people from purchasing property in certain neighborhoods, usually neighborhoods with higher property values or purchasing property overall. Property values are linked to property taxes. Property taxes are linked to education and resources available. Do you see the link?

In the *Jim Crow of the North* documentary,[25] the impact of redlining and racial covenants is explained, including the racial policies and practices encouraged via these covenants and maps. One example is the specific language that was included in property deeds, designed to be restrictive in nature. The language stated that the property could not be sold to African Americans and other minority groups. Although slavery was abolished in 1865 and Jim Crow laws were known to persist in the South from around 1870 to 1965, these practices took place in the North during this same time, hence the name Jim Crow of the North. These practices were enforced until the late 1960s.

Post-1960, unfavorable practices continued via subprime lending tactics, despite the Fair Housing Act of 1968, which essentially prohibited discrimination in the sale, rental, or financing of housing. So why am I discussing land and homeownership? Property ownership is known to be a form of generational wealth since the property can be passed down from generation to generation.

For almost 250 years, black people were enslaved and could not own property. Then for the past 100-plus years, measures were in place to restrict or limit African Americans and other minorities from homeownership and, in essence, indirectly prevent the passing of this widely known form of generational wealth. This is only one small example of how the residue of slavery continues to impact us today.

No, we did not own slaves and we were not slaves, but we must address the generational wealth and impact that many white Americans have as a result of having an almost 250-year head start, followed by another 100-plus years of inequality and unfair practices. I understand that this is not the case for every single white person, but it is disproportionately the case. No, you did not own slaves and I was not a slave, but have you benefited indirectly from the practice? This is America's history, and whether we like it or not, it does and should matter to all Americans.

Discussion Questions

- Are you positively impacted by generational wealth?
- Do you think wealth should be distributed to those who did not get generational wealth?
- Do you know your ancestry as it ties back to the years of slavery? What does it reveal?

Question #2: I don't see color, so why does this apply to me?

We were intentionally created with different skin hues. Diversity is the outward display of God's beautiful workmanship. From the intricate internal anatomy to the external physical features, we are all beautiful. To deny seeing this beauty is to deny God's creation and intentional design.

This question, though often well-intended, is out of place. The reality is, we cannot hide the color of our skin and as an African American woman, I do not want you to avoid seeing any part of me, including the color of my skin. My skin relates to a big part of who I am. Many other African Americans share the same sentiments.

When someone says they don't see color, I hear them saying they don't see me, or at least they do not see a large part of me! Not seeing my color suggests to me that you are choosing not to see a part of me or my identity. I do not want to be half seen. I want everyone to see me, in whole, for who I am.

The *I do not see color* statement also indirectly invalidates some of my experiences as a part of my identity. Often, a person who does not believe that they see color also may question experiences had by a person of color. Do you think that store clerk followed you because you are black? Maybe it was a coincidence. Did that restaurant really refuse to seat you because you are black? Did that person say it to you in that tone or are you mistaken? Often, a person who does not "see color" has a hard time processing the racial experiences of people of color.

This comment may also suggest that you don't believe racial discussions should take place since you, after all, do not see color. So not only are you suggesting that your sense of sight is off, but you may unintentionally be suggesting that another one of your five senses is turned off ... the ability to hear. If you cannot see my color, you will not hear me talk about experiences as a woman of color.

Indirectly related to you not seeing my color and hearing my stories, you may not be able to understand what you cannot see or hear. I don't want you to not see or hear me! I want you to see me ... see my color, hear me as I discuss what my color means to me, hear the experiences I have had based on my color, and understand who I am (including the who, what, when, where, how, and why)! I also want to see you and hear your story... all of it.

In the historic 1963 "I Have a Dream Speech,"[26] Reverend Dr. Martin Luther King Jr. stated, "I have a dream that my four little children will one day live in a nation where they will not be judged by the color of their skin, but by the content of their character."

I have heard this quote used to justify not seeing color. Do not take this powerful quote out of context to mean that Dr. King is saying do not see color. He didn't say don't see my color, he said do not judge me by my color. While I don't know his intentions, when studying the works of Dr. King, I am convinced that he was perfectly fine with his skin color and just wanted to be treated fairly and equally.

I urge you to read this speech in full, as many of the statements made in this speech remain applicable today. I also encourage you to read "Letters from a Birmingham Jail," written when he was imprisoned during the civil rights movement.[27]

In the aftermath of the death of George Floyd, I began to dialogue on social media with my friends about race and racial ideology, a lot of which inspired the writing of this book. A white childhood friend I hadn't seen since high school reached out on Facebook to ask for advice on talking to her toddler about race.

She admitted that she had heard mixed reviews on teaching children to be color-blind and wanted my perspective. I encouraged her to avoid the color-blind discussion and suggested that she read a Sesame Street book, *We are Different, But the Same.* It's a powerful book that I even encourage adults to read. It takes the approach of what I believe those who say, "I don't see color" intend to communicate. The book outlines how our differences are the same and are all valuable, despite being differences.

Not seeing color does not simply erase all the historical trauma associated with color. If someone is in a wheelchair and you assert that you don't see the wheelchair, it does not change the fact that they need the wheelchair for mobility and may have had adverse experiences as a result of the wheelchair.

You see, it's a challenge to deny seeing color when it's so ingrained in the American psyche. As much as we may want to say we don't see color, we do. It's not about not seeing the color, but instead, it is about not allowing the color to serve as a barrier or negative attribute. It is about not allowing color to be equated with superiority or inferiority.

Seeing color and the implicit thoughts connected to color are not new discussions. I am reminded of the famous "Doll Test" initially conducted in 1940 by famous psychologists Kenneth and Mamie Clark. The purpose of their experiment was to demonstrate the effects of segregation on African American children.[28]

Four dolls were used, and their only difference was the color of their skin. The heartbreaking experiment revealed that all of the children questioned preferred the white doll solely due to skin color and overwhelmingly had positive associations about the white doll. This was true for all participants, including African American children. So even though we may want to suggest that we don't see color, these participants, some as young as four years old, saw color, and not only did they see color, they had negative associations with black.

Now, you might be thinking that was in the 1940s and that surely in 2020, eighty years later, that has changed. I wish it were true, but this experiment was performed again several times, including as recently as 2018. It received national attention in 2010 when CNN's Anderson Cooper revisited the experiment. The results, repeatedly, have been disturbingly the same.

Another visual depiction is the Privilege Walk, which is an exercise created by Peggy McIntosh in her article entitled "White Privilege: Unpacking the Invisible Knapsack."[29] This exercise is designed to have a group come together and a facilitator reads a series of questions. The group starts in a line, shoulder to shoulder. The facilitator reads the questions, one by one, and if a question applies to you, you take a step forward. You do this after each question. At the end of the exercise, participants then have a visual depiction of how some seemingly trivial statements can set us apart and allow some to move ahead while others are left behind. A sample question is "You grew up in a house owned by your parents." If this applied to you, you would take a step forward. I encourage you to either complete the exercise or watch one of the many popular video depictions of the exercise on YouTube.

Another experiment related to color was conducted by Jane Elliott, who became widely known for her 1968 Brown eye, Blue eye experiment, which was conducted the day after Dr. Martin Luther King Jr. was assassinated. This initial experiment, also called a class divided, was designed to teach an all-white class of elementary-aged children about the effects of racial prejudices. Students were told that brown-eyed children are smarter, nicer, neater, and ultimately superior to those with blue eyes.

This experiment is also largely known for the 2001 recreation of the experiment with college students, also made into the documentary *The Angry Eye*. I encourage you to watch the experiments, which are widely available, including on YouTube. In the documentary, in a matter of minutes, the group made minority, because of the color of their eyes, has negative reactions to biased treatment.

The video is an eye-opener to what it is like to treat a person differently based solely on a physical feature, such as skin color. Though many white people have expressed the discomfort in watching this video, I challenge you to push through the discomfort. The students in these videos walked away from the experiment back into the comfortable space of reality in their white skin. Unfortunately, these feelings persist with black people and minorities every single day, and we cannot change the color of our skin. We walk in this reality every day.

One year for our annual office Christmas party, the planning committee requested that employees submit baby photos. We were not informed about what they planned to do with the photos, but I complied and submitted my photo. On the day of the party, we learned that the photos were a part of an icebreaker game. Submitted photos flashed across the overhead projector and we were challenged to match the baby picture with the employee. Whoever got the most correct won the game.

I was the only African American photo submitted. Based on our low number of African American female employees with the same skin complexion as mine, it was not a challenge to guess that the brown-skinned baby in the photo was me. In that moment, I felt a little uncomfortable, but my colleagues and I joked about who my photo could possibly be. Had I known the intended use of the photo, I would not have submitted it. The photo icebreaker was a cute idea and I enjoyed playing along, but one thing is certain … in that moment, everyone playing the game had no choice but to see my color.

Colorism in itself is pervasive in the African American community. Skin colors and hues are wide and varied. In the black community, different skin tones have different associations. As I type this, I cringe at typing black … who even decided to call us black? Our tones range from light yellow, to mahogany, to, yes, beautiful black.

I know that all colors are beautiful, including black, but society has been taught to associate the word black or dark with evil and white with purity. Black cats, blacklisted, black sheep of the family, you see where I am going with this. In the black community, associations, comparisons, and division are frequently made by light- versus dark-skinned black people.

It is said that white people are more inclined to accept lighter or "fairer" skinned blacked people. Yes, fairer-skinned. Light-skinned has been called fairer-skinned. Who coined this comparison, and what exactly makes lighter "fairer"? You are pretty for a dark-skinned girl! A side comment like that suggests that most dark-skinned girls are not pretty, so you … you are the exception. Darker-skinned black people are seen as more of a threat, where the lighter-skinned black people are presumed to be safe.

Because of the presumption of safety that accompanies lighter skin, many black people with skin light enough to be white were known to associate with being white. The concept is known as passing. Passing has been the center of many studies and documentaries. Apparently, the people who chose to pass knew that the color of their skin was seen and had power, so they chose to use their white skin to their advantage. Passing still takes place in 2020.

As a mother of two little boys who have noticeably different skin colors despite the same mother and father, I do not like the differentiations many make about my boys. I love both boys. They are both handsome. They are both beautiful. Yet in the past two years, not one week has gone by that attention hasn't been drawn to their different skin tones. How is your baby so much darker than everyone else? Where does your baby get his chocolate color? Or I just love your chocolate baby.

If people do not see color, why do they point out their different skin tones, whether good or bad intentioned? People not only see the different colors of my boys, but they are comfortable in commenting on or questioning me about the differences. I do not like it when people say things like, I love your chocolate baby and his smooth skin because my older son, four years older than his baby brother, is lighter-skinned and he hears these comments. I don't want him to presume that his lighter skin is not beautiful, nor do I want him to presume dark is an issue.

I also dislike the fact that despite his heart, my youngest son will, by the very darker hue of his skin, have different experiences in life than his brother and father, whether good or bad. I look at my boys, I see their smiles, I see their eyes, I know their hearts, but others look at my boys and they see caramel and chocolate.

This skin color division stems back to slavery. There is history about how and why light shades began to appear, but it was common for the lighter-skinned slaves to be house slaves and the darker-skinned slaves to be field slaves. History confirms that the house slaves were often raped. We know by the very nature of genetics that somewhere at some point, there was some mingling for the lighter shades to exist.

Science proves that white and white makes white. If any person has a hinge of color, somewhere, there was a mixing with black. This example is demonstrated in the story of Sally Hemings, a slave of mixed race, whose DNA proves she had children with slave owner and past President Thomas Jefferson.[30]

The result is Thomas Jefferson having a lineage of grandchildren who look like me, many of whom frequently speak out about history and their lineage. A video went viral on July 6, 2020, when black descendants of Thomas Jefferson visited Monticello and spoke out on the *TODAY Show*.[31]

Another related response is that even if you see color, you do not see race because there is only one race, the human race. I cannot disagree with this. Yes, we are one race, but we cannot deny that the human race created something called racism. For those who say race is a social construct, my response is that racism is also a social construct, which we still undeniably have issues with in America. Even if biologically we are one race, the human race, we live with experiences that have caused differentiation.

Christian civil rights leader Dr. John Perkins said, "[E]ven though race might be a socially manufactured idea, it has had a very real impact on our lives."[32] The simple "What can I do" question suggests that we all know there are differences that must be addressed, many of which are based on the color of our skin. The talk about being an ally also suggests that something has caused division and the ultimate need for an ally!

The *I don't see color* comment does not take into account the subconscious and implicit associations our minds are conditioned to make, both negative and positive associations. The media and life experiences have contributed to our mindsets. The next chapter will further expound on implicit biases and associations.

There is beauty and value in seeing the diversity of colors. If you are a Christian and believe in the Trinity, there is diversity in the very foundation of Christianity, with the Father, the Son, and the Holy Spirit. Diversity is beautiful, and we should embrace and celebrate it! It is ok for you to see color, just be sure to value the beauty of all colors and do not let seeing the color adversely impact your thoughts.

Discussion Questions

- How is your life impacted by the color of your skin? Is it adverse or positive?
- What would this world be like if we were all the same?
- Do you recall your first interaction with someone of a different skin tone?

Question #3: I'm not racist, and when examining my heart, it's clean. I love everyone with the same love of Christ, so how does this apply to me?

Racism is defined as "a belief that race is the primary deter-minant of human traits and capacities and that racial differ-ences produce an inherent superiority of a particular race."[33] Racists prescribe to this definition in their thoughts and actions. When one does not agree with these state-ments, they commonly declare, "I am not racist." Many add, "I love everyone." It is amazing that many of us, as human beings, understand the love that Christ has shown to us, starting with the ultimate show of love ... Christ dy-ing on the cross for our sins. As such, I believe whole-heart-edly that many of us may not intentionally possess adverse racial intentions in our hearts and minds. Many of us may not believe ourselves to be racist. However, simply not be-ing a racist may not be sufficient.

Unfortunately because of the world we live in and largely based on the sin problem in the world, including the history of slavery, we cannot control implicit biases and cultural awareness deficiencies we may have stemming from the biases ingrained from history and media influ-ences.

The Ohio State University's Kirwan Institute for the Study of Race and Ethnicity gives an excellent definition of implicit bias:

> [Implicit bias] refers to the attitudes or stereo-types that affect our understanding, actions, and decisions in an unconscious manner. These bi-ases, which encompass both favorable and

unfavorable assessments, are activated involuntarily and without an individual's awareness or intentional control. Residing deep in the subconscious, these biases are different from known biases that individuals may choose to conceal for the purposes of social and/or political correctness. Rather, implicit biases are not accessible through introspection.

Others are related to the media and life's exposure and experiences. We all have implicit biases, and this does not make us bad people. Implicit biases are the immediate feelings or assumptions you have about people. Implicit biases likely relate to your upbringing and life experiences. You typically may have positive biases toward those in your in-group or those most like you, but negative biases toward those not like you. The solution to minimizing the impact of our implicit biases is to become aware of our implicit biases and how they impact us.

Here are a few examples:

1. Judging a person by their name. For example, my name is LaToya. When reading my name, subconsciously, you would presume I am African American. If my name was Larry, you would presume I am a male. If you have any biases against African Americans (or men), your implicit biases may cause you to indirectly associate those biases with me. This may adversely impact me when applying for jobs and overall, in the workplace.

2. You are a waiter and you have been told that black people do not tip, so your implicit bias causes you to have an attitude and provide poor service. As a black woman who always tips 20% even when service is poor, I am discouraged by this bias. I have responded to this argument in the past by asking, "Do you think they did not tip well because they are black or because they received poor service?" The bias causes servers not to want to wait on a black table or you do so with a subconscious sense of unhappiness that is displayed in your service.

3. All Asians are smart and good at math. This bias, though on its face seemingly positive, makes a presumption and suggests that an Asian person is educated and prioritizes education over other aspects of life. This may impact the kind of assignments and work given to an Asian person.

4. Men are better musicians. This is a bias. There is a study where orchestras began having blind auditions.[34] Once this process began, the number of women getting selected was said to increase, suggesting that an implicit bias was preventing women from being selected.

5. Women are emotional and nurturing. This implicit bias may cause you to give certain duties to women, usually lower-level duties, which prevent promotion and upward mobility in companies.

Often related to implicit bias is the discussion of microaggressions and passive-aggressive language. I encourage you to dig deeper and take a training on microaggressions to ensure you are not unintentionally presenting a bias. One example is asking certain questions that suggest inferiority. Where are you from? This question, if asked to a minority of obvious African or Asian descent, may suggest that you presume they were not born in America.

"Oh, you are from Maryland!" people often respond to Dr. Odette Harris, the first black female professor of neurosurgery in the US. She explained how she has seen and experienced racism firsthand.[35] Dr. Harris explained that in response to her name card in a meeting, someone asked her if the medical doctor MD was an abbreviation for the state of Maryland.[36] How common is it for a person to put their state abbreviation after their name? Not too common. Despite the uncommon practice, the person thought it more logical to presume that she was from Maryland as opposed to presuming that she was a medical doctor. Dr. Harris said the mistake was all too common. As a lawyer (JD) with my MBA, I am so happy that JD and MBA are not the abbreviations for any states.

Harvard University has a website that allows users to take Implicit Association Tests,[37] known as an IAT test. These tests are free and include a wide array of topics, such as age, gender, religion, race, sexuality, and other areas of our lives where implicit biases persist. I encourage you to take a few of the tests and examine your results.

There are also many other resources about implicit bias that you can explore. We all have implicit biases, and with intentionality, we can become aware of these and work toward diminishing them. Another resource is the Intercultural Development Inventory (IDI). It's a "cross-cultural assessment of intercultural competence that is used by thousands of individuals and organizations to build intercultural competence to achieve international and domestic diversity and inclusion goals and outcomes."[38] This tool is commonly used in employment and other group settings.

A few years ago, I was on a panel at work. Before the panel, our American Sign Language (ASL) interpreter approached me asking for an outline of the discussion.

When I explained that the panel wasn't scripted, he said, "You all scare me because you guys are known to use big words."

I responded, "You will do fine—you always do."

This comment, from my lens, was sincere. For years, I've wanted to learn American Sign Language. After the meeting, he approached me with watery eyes and informed me that I offended him. I clutched my chest and with a confused look said, "What, how, when—what did I do?"

He explained that I dismissed his role as being insignificant. This was not at all my intent, so I, too, with tears in my eyes, explained that it was not my intention and affirmed my respect for him and our ASL community overall. He explained that it was offensive because he had been messing up a little and reminded me that when he messes up, those who rely on his interpreting don't get the message. Wow! A well-needed wake-up call for me.

Although offending him was not my intention, it stuck with me, and I am fully aware and alert when making comments and dealing with others who I differ from in any way at all, every single day. I thanked him for boldly informing me. He could have kept quiet and dealt with me with an attitude, but he didn't. I hope he knew my heart and knew it wasn't my intent, but despite my heart and intent, in that moment, his feelings were valid.

On another occasion, I heard this same person tell another black woman, who wore her hair curly and in its natural state, "Why don't you wear your hair nice and straight like LaToya?" I took the time, not in a tit for a tat manner, but from an accountability position, to let him know how that comment could be seen as offensive and rooted to biases about what straight hair actually means.

You see, straight hair is a European cultural identity that has been itself imposed as a sign of beauty, even though most black women do not have naturally straight hair. His comment was insensitive and uninformed, despite this seemingly well-meaning comment and seemingly kind compliment to me.

As another example, a previous white male supervisor felt the need to call me T (which I never approved) and would say "heeeey girllll" every time he saw me. I tried to ignore it until one day he told me via email that he planned to call me to "go all sister girl" on a coworker he disagreed with.

I immediately responded in a very professional tone and said, "I am sorry. I do not know what you are referencing because I have never gone 'sister girl' on anyone in my life. In fact, I am not sure what that means."

He immediately said, "I am sorry."

But where did this come from? What were the biases he exhibited that related to black women? Why was this ok?

When I was in law school, one of my black classmates told me he had never dealt one on one with a white woman in his life and, as a result, had a hard time understanding what one of our white female professors was teaching.

I said, "She is speaking English. What don't you understand?"

With a serious face, he insisted that he did not understand her. How is it possible that a black man in America couldn't understand a white woman? He explained that his K-12 education and Morehouse college years never included a white female teacher or professor. Wow! How? As such, this was a barrier and caused him to not be able to engage in the course. He did not perform as well in the class as he should have, despite his clear knowledge of the subject matter. He could not see past his implicit biases associated with her skin color.

As an educator, I use that experience as a lesson. I start all of my college classes with this story. Why? As a black female professor, I do not want any of my students who may have never had a black professor or teacher before to have any barriers to success, especially one as trivial as an implicit bias because of the color of my skin. I want them to know that I am a human being. I upfront debunk all myths and biases that may exist in their minds about black women.

I tell them I am not angry and that I am approachable. I remind them that I speak English and, most of all, I want to see them succeed! Often this results in a few giggles and, ultimately, serves as an icebreaker, but I have also learned that this talk sometimes is needed for my students of color who also may have never had a professor who looked like me.

One semester, I co-taught a Psychology of Racism seminar and a white student told me that before college, he had never seen a black person in person. He said as a child, he initially presumed the black people he saw on television were simply dirty white people. How could this student, born and raised in America, not know about different races and skin colors as a child? This student's lack of awareness also framed his future thinking.

In this same class, the student openly stated that our university should not have programming targeting minority students. He explained that since they are such a small percentage of the student population, we should not allocate resources to those students or supporting programs. He ended by saying that black students should attend black colleges and universities. While this comment did not take into consideration other minorities, I then thought I had a brilliant follow-up question.

I asked, "So are you presuming that we should not have ASL interpreters in classes and other large settings since our deaf student population is really small?"

Without hesitation, he said, "That is different. They do not have a choice and do not have targeted colleges for them."

It seemed to me that his biases were targeted toward black people. I invited him to coffee to continue the dialogue, an invitation he never accepted or declined.

In June 2020, a local Minneapolis news station, KSTP, led by minority reporter and producer Brandi Powell and Joshua Cobb, launched a series called "Conversations About Racism and the Road to Equality." In the first episode of the series, one of their featured guests, a white female in her mid-forties, discussed growing up in a rural predominately white town.

She stated:

> Everything I knew about black people I learned
> from TV, which looking back was really strange
> to me because it was such a white community,
> and yet I remember on local news there was a lot
> about crime and about black people and drugs
> and gangs. Looking back, I'm like, where in the
> world was any of that coming from? Because the
> community was just so homogenous, and so
> that's where that was where I learned about
> black people was the news and TV.[39]

She said her perception of African Americans, shaped
by what she saw on TV, caused her to fear African Americans. This story was all too familiar to me. It made me think
about the power of cultural competence and awareness.

Cultural competence refers to one's ability to interact
effectively with people of different cultures and/or socioeconomic backgrounds. It is being aware of cultures and
norms that differ from your own. Now it doesn't just stop
with awareness but also relates to your attitude toward
those different cultural components.

When someone speaks about becoming culturally competent, they are referencing the need to acknowledge, understand, accept, and interact with people across different
cultures in a positive way. I charge everyone to learn about
cultural competency and awareness, implicit biases, and
microaggressions. Microaggressions are comments that are
seemingly appropriate, but at their root, are negative undertones and slightly derogatory toward people of

minority or oppressed groups. These comments, often said in casual discussion, are largely offensive.

Let me tell you a story. Take a deep breath and imagine the following scene. Police cars are racing toward a public park. Word is out that there was a shooting at the local park involving children. The perpetrators, wearing white T-shirts, fled the scene, but two children were shot. The neighborhood is in an uproar. One mother just learned that her child was fatally shot. She yelled to the top of her lungs, "No, not my baby," as she was comforted by her boyfriend. Take another deep breath.

Here is another story. Imagine this next scene. The local golf course holds summer camp sessions to introduce neighborhood children to the game of golf. During the first day of camp, one of the children went into cardiac arrest. The child's health identification card confirmed his adverse health history. He did not survive the unfortunate occurrence, despite the golf instructor's resuscitation attempts. The child's parent's secretaries were immediately notified. Upon arriving at the hospital, in tears, the parents quietly embraced one another.

Take one final deep breath. Answer the following questions:

Story 1:

1. What was the gender of the perpetrators who fled the park?
2. How did the perpetrators look?
3. What was the color of the perpetrator's skin?
4. What was the skin color of the children shot?

Story 2:

1. What was the gender of the child who died?
2. How did the golf instructor look?
3. What was the color of the golf instructor's skin?
4. What was the skin color of the child who died?

Now be honest with yourself in reflecting on these answers. Did your mind immediately suggest skin colors for characters in the stories? What were the skin colors? Why did your mind associate the shooting with that skin color? Why did your mind associate the golf course setting with that skin color? Was the same skin color associated with each story? Why or why not? While we may not believe that we see color, our minds subconsciously make associations and presumptions that include race. Those presumptions are linked to our implicit biases.

A coworker once congratulated me on a promotion by saying, "I am happy you have that role because no one will challenge you." When I asked why, he said "You are scary. No one would dare not submit work to you."

Confused and offended, I politely asked him when I had ever done anything to make him fear me or feel that I was scary.

He cleaned it up and said, "You know what I mean. You are such a good worker and are so organized and efficient, and that intimidates me, so I presume it intimidates others."

This coworker took an opportunity to turn a compliment into an insult. That day, I felt discouraged. I wondered if he had called me scary or intimidating to anyone else? I try so hard not to be perceived as an angry black woman, but his comment, unwarranted, put me right in the very place I did not want to be in! I spent the next few days critically examining how I show up. Do my intentional actions matter, or will the color of my skin and implicit biases always win?

You are so well-spoken. You are a pretty black woman. You dress so well. You are always so put together. These are other examples of comments that may seem like compliments but can be viewed as microaggressions. Bottom line, we must educate ourselves about microaggressions.

One final suggestion is that sometimes not being racist is simply not enough. Not being racist does not require a call to action. It simply is a self-affirming statement that does not have the power to change others or outcomes. A different term suggested is anti-racist as opposed to not racist. An anti-racist may take conscious affirmative actions or inactions to prevent racism.

One of the very things an anti-racist can do is speak out and be vocal about racial inequities. An anti-racist can and should be bold! Declaring that you are not a racist is great! Following the biblical command to love requires you to take a stance against racism. Doing something to prevent racial injustices is necessary! Do not only say you are not a racist but let your actions demonstrate the heart of an anti-racist.

Discussion Questions

- What is one implicit bias you have?
- Why should cultural competence and awareness matter?
- Have you ever issued or experienced a microaggression?

Question #4: Why do Diversity and Inclusion initiatives, and race discussions in general, focus on black and white when there are many other races, cultures, and minority groups?

It's undeniable that much of the physical foundation and infrastructure of America were largely built on the backs of slaves or as a result of slavery, or the abolishing thereof. The fact that slaves were stolen from Africa and brought to America, forced into the servitude that we know historically as slavery, warrants discussion.

You see, while there are certainly other oppressed groups in America, black people are not immigrants. We did not voluntarily migrate to America. We were brought here with the intent of being property and machinery. The conditions that black people were brought to America under, in their very nature, were inhumane. Chained together on disease infested boats, many did not survive the capture trip.

We were treated and sold as property. In fact, the 1857 *Dred Scott* case defined us as property and not people.[40] The justification for slavery, from a moral lens, was that we were not viewed as human. These very facts cause different issues and discussions to dominate. Imagine yourself being raped or watching a loved one be raped. Psychologically, where would experiencing or witnessing that trauma put you?

As stated in the brief history chapter, many laws stem directly from the desire to keep African American people enslaved and not viewed as human. This desire resulted in a civil war a little over 150 short years ago. Post-Civil War, laws and systematic oppressions continue to operate in our everyday lives. Now, to say that black history is important does not diminish other history. Other racial groups' history is important and warrants attention, reflection, memory, and respect. The ultimate common goal is to dismantle racism and oppression for everyone, but it does not change the very fact that many racial issues in America, due to the sheer history, relate to black and white.

In diversity trainings, it is common for the black and white issues to dominate, and I have personally participated in trainings where non-black minorities have indicated the feeling of being unheard due to the dominance and attention given to black and white issues. It's indisputable that black issues may differ from issues of other minority groups, and other minority groups may also have unique issues. I strongly encourage any organization seeking to improve on diversity and inclusion to have subgroups where every voice can feel heard.

This issue also stems beyond just race, but also to gender. I have often heard black women indicate that their issues are slightly different than that of a black man. Black women are double minorities, being both black and female. For example, a common issue with black women is hair, and the common misperception is that of the angry black woman.

Now, I understand that hair issues can relate to black men as we talk about dreadlocks and hair, but often, there are slightly differentiated issues. The dreadlock discussion makes me think about Bob Marley. It is ironic how nationwide people love Bob Marley and his music. Many retail stores are known to play Bob Marley as the background music in their stores. Reggae music is associated with happiness and the happiness causes a desire to shop. People vacation to Jamaica and embrace the music, food, and culture, which includes the dreadlocks that Bob Marley and local natives wear. Yet, those same dreadlocks are viewed as a threat once the vacation ends. Why is that?

The hair issue has been given national attention, and many states are now passing Crown Acts[41] to prevent discrimination against a person wearing their hair in styles that complement the way their hair naturally grows from their scalps.

I also encourage companies to truly examine their diversity and inclusion policies, initiatives, and intent. It has been suggested that diversity quotas are now being met by white women. I am a woman through and through, and I know the struggles that women have and continue to face in America, from the pay gap and glass ceiling to other issues faced with having to sometimes choose between being full-time homemakers and caregivers or career-driven.

We see this now with COVID-19 as mothers are balancing home and work without school or childcare. I am in no way diminishing the work and need for equality for women, but I encourage companies to ensure that their diversity practices are broad and inclusive. This includes intentional planning to ensure that all diversity components are fulfilled and not simply overshadowed with programs for select minority groups.

Some history related to this is the creation and expansion of the use of people of color. Now, there is some history to "colored" in itself, as it was heavily used to reference black people in a derogatory way during the time of segregation. It's not common for a black person to see a positive association with the word colored. I view a person as uniformed and behind the times if I am referenced as a colored person. It makes me think about the Colored Only sections during the Jim Crow era.

The resurgence of the word colored is now used in a different context to include a broader group of minorities. People of color include any minority group or everyone who is not white. This is often used as a tool to diminish the true diversity present and began being used within the last twenty years. Also, it is out of place, as white is also a color.

Another thought about diversity and inclusion is the second word in this phrase, inclusion. I would encourage every organization to reevaluate its D&I initiatives to ensure that the work doesn't stop with simply hiring for "diversity" only but continue by ensuring that those hired feel included in the workplace. Inclusive cultures require work and intentional efforts, which require open and honest discussions about race, bias (explicit and implicit), and overall cultural competency and awareness.

It has been said that people don't leave jobs—they leave cultures, and unfortunately, those cultures are often toxic or non-inclusive. The focus on black is not designed to suppress others. I challenge you to improve your cultural competency and learn about all cultures.

In the aftermath of the death of George Floyd, many changes are taking place, including the change of mottos, symbols, the need for public statements about companies and their stance on race, and the need for intentional plans to ensure inclusive environments. Many of these discussions are stemming from the protests, the Black Lives Matter movement, and now vocal employees and consumers.

People are now boldly calling out racial occurrences, policies, and practices. Not only is it impacting businesses, but many churches are being faced with the request to speak into the narratives being presented about race. What is the role of the Church? The role is not to be quiet. The role is to lead the charge. The role is to be more Christ-like and be peacemakers, which means having these bold discussions to get to a place of peace.

Other current events are being broadcasted, and people are making insensitive comments on social media or being recorded doing so. Many companies are displaying zero tolerance, and the result has been people being fired in response to their comments or behaviors.

In June 2020, Amy Cooper threatened to call the police on birdwatcher Christian Cooper when he asked her to put her dog on a leash in Central Park, per the rules. She threatened to call the police and tell them an African American man was threatening her life. The video went viral, and in the aftermath, Cooper was fired from her job at Franklin Templeton. The company made a public statement that they have a zero-tolerance policy for racism.

In May 2020, a Florida mother attempted to drown her autistic son but falsely reported him as missing. She lied in her police report and specifically stated that two black men abducted her son. However, surveillance footage documented her pushing her son into a local canal.

What do these two examples have in common? Both women knew the power of blaming black men. Amy Cooper didn't just indicate she would say a man was threatening her, but an African American man. The Florida killer knew saying black men would deflect attention from her to the alleged black abductors. Would these dynamics have differed if the accusers would have said another race or no race at all? If Amy Cooper had said a white man was threatening her life, would the reaction or power have differed?

The media has portrayed African Americans in a certain adverse light, and the result has warranted special attention to be given to black and white issues. This is demonstrated in the 1915 controversial film *Birth of a Nation*. The movie, originally called *The Clansman*, was known to be the first film of its length ever made. This black and white movie is known for multiple controversial topics but is heavily known for the characters, including one dressed in blackface who played an African American man. Controversially, the film depicted this black man as uneducated and suggested that the was inclined to be sexually interested in and unsafe for the white woman, who was portrayed as a damsel in distress.

The movie ends by showing the white woman as afraid and believing that the African American man is going to rape her. She is saved by white men who ride in to her rescue wearing white cape-like sheets. This very movie and mindset have continued to be reflected in how we engage, whether intentionally or not. Amy Cooper knew the power of saying that an African American man was threatening her life.

In *White Fragility* by Robin DiAngelo, DiAngelo has a chapter entitled "White Women's Tears," and she discusses the power dynamics and historical connections to a white woman and her tears. Overall, American history includes the ugly story of racism, and that cannot be erased. A remnant is the elevation of black and white issues that persist in our American society. This naturally causes black and white issues to dominate discussions.

A related question is why is there a black history month? We don't have a white history month. Here is the short answer ... Every month is white history month. The history books used depict white history. Many of these books fail to include black history, which is a large part of America's history. In America, the overall culture accepted is heavily influenced by white history. The news media, companies, and overall influence is from the white perspective.

Black History Month, officially recognized in 1976, stemmed from Negro History Week. I recall as a child the joke about us not only being given one month, but the shortest month of the twelve. Despite this comic relief, ideally, we will eventually get to a place where the narrative does not have to be so black and white. The hope is to get to a place where all colors are valued and celebrated.

Discussion Questions

- What is your racial/cultural identity and how does it impact you?
- How do you feel about diversity and inclusion?
- How has the media shaped your perception about race?

Question #5: All Lives Matter, so why do we say Black Lives Matter?

Should All Lives Matter? Absolutely. I don't think any black person who supports the Black Lives Matter statement would suggest otherwise. The history of race relations in America, specifically with black people, has clearly suggested that all lives do not matter. From slavery to all forms of systematic oppression, including, but not limited to, police brutality, it feels like black lives either don't matter or are seen as less valuable.

When a person says All Lives Matter, it is largely viewed as dismissive and disrespectful. All Lives Matter is a microinvalidation. Yes, the ultimate goal is for us to get to a place where All Lives Matter, but until we get to that time, we have to continue to elevate our voice and bring awareness to the reason behind the hashtag statement #BlackLivesMatter. The history and purpose of Black Lives Matter, retrieved directly from their website, states:

> #BlackLivesMatter was founded in 2013 in response to the acquittal of Trayvon Martin's murderer. Black Lives Matter Foundation, Inc. is a global organization in the US, UK, and Canada, whose mission is to eradicate white supremacy and build local power to intervene in violence inflicted on Black communities by the state and vigilantes. By combating and countering acts of violence, creating space for Black imagination and innovation, and centering Black joy, we are winning immediate improvements in our lives.

The website further states, "We are working for a world where Black lives are no longer systematically targeted for demise."[42] Even if you don't support the cause or position of Black Lives Matter as an organization, you should distinguish the actual statement from the organization. Even if you do not support all the ideals of the organization, the statement holds truth. Many use the hashtag without intended association with the organization.

Trayvon Martin was a seventeen-year-old African American boy who was murdered in his father's gated subdivision in Florida. His killer was acquitted for his murder after he raised the argument of self-defense. Despite the 911 recorded transcript clearly having the dispatcher tell the killer, and neighborhood watch volunteer, George Zimmerman, "We don't need you to follow him," you can hear other offensive and prejudicial accusations and assumptions made by Zimmerman during the call.

Post-case, the question of whether the prosecutor properly charged Zimmerman was raised, as Zimmerman asserted self-defense under Florida's Stand Your Ground statute. Fast-forward, many were outraged when a picture went viral with George Zimmerman and a bag of Skittles that he autographed. The photo also had a confederate flag as the background…. yes, that confederate flag.

When Trayvon Martin was murdered, he had Skittles in the pocket of his hoodie, and while he is dead, his killer is seemingly being glorified and signing a bag of Skittles, possibly the last thing that Trayvon ate. This is why we have to differentiate and focus on black lives and remind the world that Black Lives Matter!

In the wake of the death of George Floyd, many began to post All Lives Matter. For some, it was intentional and for others, they thought the post was a sign of support and inclusiveness. Many examples began to circulate on social media explaining why All Lives Matter is out of place. Here is one example:

The Sheep Example

In the parable of the lost sheep, written in Luke 15, Jesus cares about the one sheep that is different or in need. Of course, Jesus cares about and loves all sheep, and he knew that all sheep mattered, but because he loved them all, he went back for the one left behind because that lost sheep mattered too!

I often wonder if people would have a challenge with understanding Black Lives Matter if the original hashtag said #BlackLivesMatterToo or #BlackLivesMatterAlso. Bottom line, Black Lives Matter, and before we can inclusively say that All Lives Matter, we have to see that Black Lives Matter. As long as black lives continue to be seen as less valuable and suggestively not matter, we cannot make a fully inclusive statement that All Lives Matter because the facts of how black people are treated in America, now and historically, says otherwise. Here is another example:

The Burning House Example

Let's presume that your house is on fire and that it is obviously burning and is the only house on fire on the block. The fire department shows up and decides to spray water on all houses on the block and gives limited attention to your burning house that really needs the water. What if you said, "Hey, my house is on fire—give it more water. My house matters." The firefighter then responds and says, "All houses matter."

This is exactly what it feels like when we hear, All Lives Matter! Yes, all houses do matter, but in that moment, your house is on fire … and with all the injustices black people are experiencing, we feel like we are on fire, being destroyed the same way fire destroys! We are simply asking for the fire to be extinguished, and since our issues are literally in need of attention, we need more water.

Other examples include responding to a specific cancer fundraiser with the comment, "All cancer matters," or telling a bereaved family, "I, too, have experienced a loss." A final example is in reference to the eight beatitudes in Matthew 5:3-12. Saying All Lives Matter would be like responding to the beatitudes with all-inclusive statements.

Blessed are the poor in spirit … would the response to this one or any of the other seven beatitudes be, "No, Lord, blessed is everyone"? The singular act of pointing out these eight groups does not negate the blessing of any other group. These examples show that the focus on one thing does not mean that other things are excluded or not of focus. The examples continue, but the use of All Lives Matter also continues.

In the aftermath of the death of George Floyd, I have seen the statement made, some intentionally, sending the tone and message, "Stop yelling Black Lives Matter," to the tone of, "Yes, we value black lives, but we also value all lives." The goal is to get to the place where we can just simply say All Lives Matter, but we as a country, and individually, have work to do before that can be said with confidence. An ideal place is where not even All Lives Matter is needed because it is just understood to be the case.

Another example related to the All Lives Matter response is any time one feels the need to deflect the attention from black lives and draw attention to other issues or injustices. As the examples above demonstrate, we can give attention to more than one issue at a time.

During COVID-19, many churches began to have virtual services. I attended a Facebook Live church service and the topic, fitting for the mid-June 2020 date, was about justice and having uncomfortable conversations about race and Black Lives Matter. I was likely one of maybe five people of color on the stream.

As we were engaging via the chat feature, one of the participants commented, "The real injustice in the world today is abortion. Over 1 million lives murdered in the US every year." A year ago, I am not sure I would have responded, but the new bold me said, "No more." I encourage every reader to not only be bold but to specifically call out injustices, racial comments, and overall inappropriately-timed comments, whether intentionally made or not, every single time they occur.

Before I could respond, someone else responded and simply said, "We can care about more than one thing at a time."

The initiator responded, "I agree."

I replied and calmly redirected his question, reminded him that Black Lives Matter, and suggested that he do some historical research on who abortion was designed to abort in the first place (a history lesson in itself, despite differing opinions).

He reverenced Margaret Sanger, and I informed him that I was well aware of Margaret Sanger and her role with the now known Planned Parenthood. I am aware of the controversial Negro Project, led by Margaret Sanger and her organization, which was designed to provide black women in the South birth control and other forms of contraceptives.

At the end of our discussion, I gave him my phone number and welcomed more dialogue. He did call me that same day. After three minutes of introductions, I cut right to the chase and explained why his comments were insensitive and misplaced. I used the examples above to demonstrate why All Lives Matter as a response is not ok. He apologized, said he is known to rock the boat, and invited me to dinner that afternoon. Although I graciously declined, I was happy that we dialogued and hope if nothing else, the seed was planted.

Though misplaced, his comments were somewhat accurate, in the sense that there are other issues and we should care about those issues as well, but in addition to Black Lives Matter, not as a replacement. Other issues make me question if all lives truly matter. The border crisis is one of the examples. As I type these words, many migrant babies and children are being detained, separate from their parents. These children are subjected to deplorable and unsanitary conditions. Human trafficking, DACA, and other issues that persist make me question if All Lives Matter. And this, then, makes me question whether the All Lives Matter response is really an issue with the word black.

All Lives Matter misses and diverts the message. All Lives Matter misses the big picture. The message and big picture is black lives are not being treated as if they matter.

If you want to get to a place where all lives truly matter, I encourage you to use your voice and platform. Hold your circles and institutions accountable for equity. If you are in a position of authority, hire people of color and ensure that they feel a sense of inclusion and belonging. If you see injustices, speak out against them.

Continue to educate yourself about history and injustices. Continue to educate yourself about different cultures and minority groups. Be a leader. Be a voice. Advocate for change. Listen to those who do not feel that Black Lives Matter. Commit to listening to anyone who says that they don't feel like their life matters. Commit to a change so we ultimately can get to a place where all lives actually matter.

Here is another related question: Why can't Africans just go back to Africa or build their own economies somewhere else? As a reminder, Africans did not voluntarily choose to come to America. My ancestors were stolen from Africa and brought to America to be enslaved and serve as free labor. We are not immigrants. Further, we are so far removed from 1619, the comment is insulting.

America is the home that many African Americans, born on American soil, know. Further, African Americans heavily contributed to the building of America that we know today. The value of a person was diminished by enslaving them for the sake of economics. I would also like to add, this statement is offensive not only because of Africans being captured and brought to America but because America was not initially inhabited by white men. As such, this argument suggests that white people should also leave America. This is a lot of history that we cannot forget. History cannot ignore the attempts at African Americans to build their own economies and wealth. As discussed in the history chapter, don't forget about Rosewood, Black Wall Street, and other attempts at economic sufficiency.

Discussion Questions

- In America, do you feel that all lives are treated with the same level of respect, value, and importance?
- Have you ever felt that your life was not valued or did not matter?
- Do you believe that more than one issue can be elevated at a time?

Question #6: If black people don't commit crimes, they will not have this issue, right?

When this comment arises, many thoughts run through my mind. I do not support anyone committing a crime and not facing punishment in accordance with the alleged wrongdoing, but only after properly being found guilty. The ideal scenario would include a punishment fitting the crime. The issue with the uproar over police injustices suggests that black people, often stopped for minor traffic infractions, are being killed in the process of the routine traffic stop.

In the Malcolm Gladwell book, *Talking to Strangers: What We Should Know about the People We Don't Know*, Mr. Gladwell opens and closes his book with the story of Sandra Bland, who was pulled over in July 2015 in Texas. Her entire confrontation with the officer was recorded via his dash camera video footage, which has been viewed millions of times on YouTube.

Gladwell includes the transcript of their dialogue exchange, which ended with Bland being arrested and jailed. Three days later, she was found dead in her cell, and the suggested cause of death was suicide. Bland was a twenty-something-year-old black woman who had just moved to Texas for a new job. She had just launched a series of inspirational videos on YouTube.

The officer said he pulled her over because she failed to signal when she changed lanes. How does a routine fail to signal traffic stop end with death? Gladwell continues by briefly outlining the police-related stops and deaths of Michael Brown, Freddie Gray, Philando Castille, Eric Gardner, and Walter Scott.

Other African American people were killed while in routine custody. George Floyd was said to be stopped for allegedly using a counterfeit twenty-dollar bill at a neighborhood store that, according to the owner, he frequented. If the money was counterfeit, he should have been arrested and charged in accordance with whatever the law states as the punishment for that crime, misdemeanor, or felony. However, he was never given that opportunity, as he was killed after being handcuffed and restrained, after numerous pleas for air because he couldn't breathe.

While police body cameras and local surveillance show the incident, even if he was resisting arrest initially, when the officer kept his knee on his neck for over eight minutes, he was not only no longer a threat, but he was handcuffed and in submission.

Philando Castille was fatally killed in July 2016 during a traffic stop. After being asked for his license and registration, he complied and told the officer he had a firearm, which he was licensed to carry. The officer said, "Don't pull it out." After clearly stating he would not, Philando was shot seven times at close range. He died on the scene. His girlfriend and her four-year-old child were in the car, and she recorded the traffic stop.

The alleged reason for pulling him over was the police's statement that the two occupants of the car looked like robbery suspects, due to the size and shape of their noses. They were mistaken. His only crimes that afternoon were going to the grocery store with his girlfriend and her child, politely informing the officer that he had a concealed weapon, that he was rightfully licensed to carry, and the shape of his nose.

I can add story after story of black men and women killed by officers, not only during routine traffic stops but many while in their homes or out for a jog or walk in the neighborhood. Remember Trayvon Martin, the teenager killed in his father's neighborhood while out walking with a hoodie on and a bag of Skittles. Have you heard of Breonna Taylor, killed in her own bed by a faulty no knock-warrant? The evidence later suggested that the warrant was to be executed over ten miles away from her apartment.

The list goes on and on. The facts show, time after time, black people being killed during police interactions, never to be given their day in court. If black people (or any person for that matter) commit crimes, they should be charged and punished accordingly. We cannot get to that point if compliant black people are killed by the very people designed to protect and serve ... the officers.

Also troubling is the seemingly different treatment given to minorities while in custody as compared to white criminals. In June 2015, killer Dylan Roof went to a Bible study at Emanuel African Methodist Episcopal Church and murdered nine African American parishioners. Not only did this mass murderer survive his police encounter and get to see his day in court, but his arrest also received national attention after the police officers allegedly brought him to Burger King for food because, after his arrest, he stated that he was hungry. I am not suggesting that Roof should not have been provided food. I am only drawing this comparison to offer my heartfelt wish that many of the black people killed could have been given similar courtesies during their fatal encounters.

Police injustice is not a new topic or issue. The incidences are now being recorded so the world can see the actions and inactions. Everyone has access to cameras, and it takes one second to click the live button and another second for something to go viral. It's the world we live in. There are now cell phone cameras, dashboard cameras, and body cameras to record the injustice, so we are all protected, right? Wrong.

We watched Philando Castille be killed and the officer not be convicted. We watched Eric Garner in 2014, killed by an officer while on the ground pleading that he could not breathe. Time and time again, the recordings suggest excessive use of force and unjustified killing, followed by delayed charging of the killers and not-guilty verdicts.

To add insult to injury, days after the death of George Floyd, Hennepin County attorney Mike Freeman defended his office and suggested that they were one of the few offices to convict a cop in a killing. He is correct. Yes, they did get a verdict for a white woman. To be crystal clear, that outcome would have likely differed if it was a black girl— let's call her LaToya—and a white or non-black cop. The verdict that Freeman boasted about was one where a Somali cop was convicted of killing a white woman.

A related question is, "Well what about black-on-black crime? Isn't that an issue?" I will briefly answer this question with two small points. First, yes, black-on-black crime is an issue, but note that when someone black kills another black person, or any other person for that matter, the black killer is arrested and charged for their crime. However, too often, the officer or killer charged (if ever charged) is not convicted for the crimes related to the death of unarmed black people.

Further, statistics show that white-on-white crime occurs at the same, or higher, rate as black-on-black crime.

This is true for any other race. Due to geographical demographics, it is prevalent for murders to be race on race. However, the media magnifies the attention given to black-on-black crimes. Why is that?

The second issue with that question suggests that the questioner is trying to justify police brutality. When the response to an issue is the presenting of another issue, as opposed to proposing or supporting a solution, the natural presumption is to see the response as defensive and not understanding the root issue.

The facts do not support the blanket uninformed and offensive comment that suggests every black person killed by a cop is first guilty of committing a crime. It is just not factual. Black-on-black crime is an issue, but so is white-on-white crime and police injustice, *bottom line*. There is nothing to suggest that we cannot have multiple issues and dismissing the problem by shifting blame creates another problem.

Another suggestion inferred from the black-on-black crime response is that the responder is saying it's ok to kill black people because black people kill black people. There is also power in the media. The picture that has been painted shows black people as violent. I will use the media example presented after Hurricane Katrina hit New Orleans, Louisiana in 2005. The news stories had powerful words to describe the content of the accompanying photographs. One photo of black people exiting an abandoned store with food identified them as looters. A similar photo of white people exiting an abandoned store with food identified them as survivors.

In talking about criminalization, we must also examine the institution of prisons, the history, and the rise of mass incarceration. The documentary *13th* paints a clear picture of mass incarceration and the impacts on minorities. The school-to-prison pipeline also impacts the criminalization of African Americans. This pipeline is a funnel where African American boys are targeted for purported behavior problems and expelled as early as at the age of four. This phenomenon largely impacts minority males, as black and Latinx males are not tolerated at the same rate as white males the same age for the same behavior issues.

There is an undeniable linkage between dropping out of school and the chances of going to prison. Further, these students often have or are labeled as having learning disabilities and histories of poverty. The students who would be prime candidates for counseling or tutoring are often punished. Because of zero-tolerance policies, they end up expelled or suspended from school.

Public attention was given to the school-to-prison pipeline when the kids-for-cash scandal was uncovered. This scandal included two judges who were accused of accepting kickback money to impose harsh sentences on juveniles and ultimately increase the population of juvenile detention centers. The increased population was an increase in profit for the centers.

In 2010, one of the judges pled guilty and was sentenced to prison time. As a result, the Pennsylvania Supreme Court overturned hundreds of juvenile sentences. The other judge opted to stand trial and was sentenced to twenty-eight years in federal prison. This scandal was explained in the 2013 documentary *Kids for Cash*.

A final example that sheds light on this false narrative has been outlined in the 2019 four-part documentary *When They See Us*, which is based on the true story of five young black boys falsely accused of raping and assaulting a white woman in New York's Central Park. These boys, known as the Central Park Five, are now men, who were exonerated after spending years in prison.

Stories like this confirm the misperception placed on African American boys. As a mother of two little African Americans boys who will grow up to be men, my heart aches to fathom my children being criminalized due to the mere color of their skin. The premise that black people should be targeted because they are criminals is a false narrative.

Discussion Questions

- Do you believe our criminal justice system has inequities toward minorities?
- Do you now believe, or have you ever believed, that one race is more violent than another race? Why?
- Do you fear interactions with police officers?

Question #7: Why can't black people simply work harder? After all, we all have access to the same freedoms here in America, right?

Wrong! History suggests that in America, civil rights are not always equally applied. I will not revisit the history lesson, but remember that for the first 250 years black people were in America, we were enslaved and forced to perform labor, for which we were not compensated. Then for nearly another 100 years, black people fought for equality, despite being over 250 years behind our white counterparts.

During this 100-year time period, which included the Jim Crow era, black people faced lynchings, bombings, assassinations, massacres, and other hate crimes, separate but equal, literacy tests to avoid basic freedoms such as voting, poll taxes, segregation, and outright hatred. When considering these events, be reminded that it was not that long ago that black bodies were lynched and hung from trees, referred to in the famous Billie Holiday song, *Strange Fruit*, as strange fruit hanging from the trees. Lynchings were not illegal until 1962. That was not too long ago. Do a Google search and you can find disturbing images from public lynches, where bystanders were present in their Sunday's best, including children.

People born during the 1950s are in their sixties. Many of these people know about these experiences firsthand, not just from historical stories. Although Jim Crow is outlawed, the very person running your organization may have been pro-Jim Crow or pro-segregation. They themselves may have been involved in the segregating of schools. If born in the 60s, 70s, or 80s, they may be the grandchild of someone who either supported or experienced segregation. We are not far removed.

Fast-forward to the time frame of 1964–2020. This is over fifty years of continuing to fight for equality and access and being suppressed in systemically oppressive ways. This lack of access and barriers relates to access to equal education, employment discrimination, housing discrimination, including redlining and restrictive covenants, mass incarceration, inequity in health care, environmental injustices, and other barriers.

Yes, many black people have worked hard. We now hold professional degrees, have increasing levels of higher education, and have accumulated wealth. Despite the wealth that a few have accumulated, statistics still confirm that the wealth gap between black and white Americans is staggering.

Historical data confirms that no progress has been made in reducing income and wealth gaps since the 1960s. Studies confirm that the gap has increased. When viewing this in the context of millionaire status, one in seven white families are now millionaires, whereas only one in fifty African Americans are millionaires.[43] This is of no surprise given the historical disadvantage and lack of opportunity to accumulate or pass down wealth.

In addition to barriers, microaggressions and implicit biases also challenge many African Americans and prevent them from overcoming. Many of these barriers, whether intentional or not, result from the sheer nature of who is in control of the most common institutions, traditionally white men.

One of the best examples I have heard was presented by author Kimberly Jones in a video that went viral days after the death of George Floyd. Jones gave a monopoly example to explain why 400 years after the first slaves were brought to America, black people remain at a significant economic disadvantage.

The monopoly example was also used over twenty-five years ago by economist Dr. Claud Anderson. Their examples clearly explain how wealth accumulates. If you equate the rounds of the game to years, the suggestion is if you played the game of Monopoly for 250 rounds and cannot own anything, then eventually you can own property, but what you own is taken, destroyed, taxed at a heavier rate, or overall more expensive to retain, then you will never be able to win.

These factors make it almost impossible to catch up or have a fair chance of competing in the game. It essentially makes the game, equated to life, impossible, unequal, and unfair for the minority group. The example is one of economics and paints the picture of how it causes even the hardest worker to be at a disadvantage.

The economics discussion is foundational as it relates to America. Historically, the value of economics has seemingly always been given more significance than some forms of life. The very nature of slavery in its inception was purely economics. People were dehumanized for monetary gain.

Fast-forward to 2020. COVID-19 caused America to go on lockdown and shelter in place. Despite rising numbers, the shelter in place ended with pressure to get back out and stimulate the economy. Some Americans were given stimulus checks. The purpose of the stimulus checks was not solely to help citizens meet financial obligations or provide basic needs such as food, but it was, as the very name states, designed to stimulate the economy. The stimulus checks were not about people, but economics.

The decision to reopen the economy, though varied by states and cities, was in many instances also controversial. The how, when, and why were heavily scrutinized. Another form of protesting began as select Americans felt that the decision to keep the economy closed, coupled with the requirements to wear masks or adhere to curfews, were in violation of their freedoms. Others have suggested that COVID-19 is not real and that mask-wearing is not effective.

I am cautious with my opinions, as I am not a medical doctor or scientist and have not studied the true impact or effects of wearing a mask or the overall COVID-19 virus. I am sensitive to the many people who have succumbed to COVID-19 and their loved ones who were left mourning their deaths.

Whether a death certificate said COVID-19 or not, if someone died during the COVID-19 pandemic from anything suggestive or related to COVID—either before or after the reopening of the economy—the decision to reopen may be suggestive that economics was placed above health and life.

The counterargument to not reopening was, *How can I survive if I cannot go to work?* The response to that argument was, *How can you go to work if you aren't alive?* Further, the country did not just suddenly reopen. Reported statistics confirmed that African American and minority communities were impacted and dying at a higher rate than any other group. After these reports, many began to push harder for the reopening of the economy.

Like any issue, different people are impacted in different ways. One specific example is St. John the Baptist Parish, located in Louisiana's cancer alley. St. John the Baptist Parish was reported to have the highest COVID-19 death rate per capita.[44] The reports suggested that this correlation was due to the presence of underlying health issues in the residents, such as cancer, hypertension, diabetes, kidney disease, and obesity. This is of no surprise given the connection to pollution and air quality in this very same community.

This community, home to many chemical plants and refineries, is known as a part of cancer alley. Cancer alley is an eighty-five mile stretch between New Orleans and Baton Rouge, Louisiana. This is an example of us not having the same access. St. John the Baptist Parish residents, heavily African American, do not have access to clean air.

Studies have confirmed that the unclean air is not only polluted but correlated to high cancer rates and the presence of cancer carcinogens. The history connects this area as one historically known to be the home of slave plantations and one to be redlined, which ultimately contributed to the interest of chemical plants to make it their home. For many in this town, their access is not equal.

There are other environmental issues, such as the Flint, Michigan water crisis. After officials repeatedly dismissed claims that Flint's water was making people sick, residents elevated their claims to the media and other platforms to prove that the water was contaminated and their overall unequal access to clean water. This included providing proof from home water samples that reflected discolored, foul-smelling, and lead-filled water.

Historically, Flint was known for a productive economy as a result of the presence of the auto industry. Flint is also known for the waste and issues with its waterways. Today, the population is more than 50% African American and almost half of its residents are at or below the poverty line. This community is fighting for equal access. Many other communities are suffering from a lack of environmental equity.

Here are other related topics that demonstrate the lack of equal access. Consider exploring these topics with your Growth Group:

1. Redlining and restrictive covenants and how these mechanisms prevented African Americans from obtaining homeownership. This topic relates to the G.I. Bill and the treatment of black soldiers returning home post-war and their lack of ability to secure homes with the G.I. Bill, despite its purpose and promise. This topic also relates to the history of how the interstate and highway systems were built strategically to accommodate the predominately white neighborhoods. Another related topic is gentrification. Finally, notice the correlation between historically redlined areas and how, ultimately, resources and access remain inequitable in and to those communities.

2. Education and the impacts thereof, including standardized testing, achievement gaps, and the role of the educator in success. This topic also includes the school-to-prison

pipeline and how the system has caused an increase in black adolescents failing to matriculate in the K-12 school system.

3. Injustices with African Americans and health care, including historical and current issues. This includes the overwhelming rate that African American women die during pregnancy and childbirth and the unequal research and support to health issues known to be more prevalent in African American and minority communities.

4. In addition to cancer alley and the Flint Michigan water crisis, other EPA and environmental-related issues and the correlation on and impact to minority communities.

All Americans do not have the same access to the same resources. We are all guaranteed the right to life, liberty, and property. However, the quality of life, liberty, and property is not created equal.

Discussion Questions

- Do you believe poor environmental conditions contribute to a lack of access or opportunities?
- Do you believe wealth accumulation is a factor that contributes positively or adversely to a person's life?
- Do you believe reparations should be given to the oppressed group?

Question #8: We had a black president and black people have good jobs and equal access. Doesn't that make everyone equal and America post-racial?

Absolutely *not*! Unfortunately, studies revealed that the racial divide in America increased when Barack Obama became President of the United States and further increased as he entered his second term. While it may be hard to factually prove, many people did not support Barack Obama purely because of the color of his skin.

A Harvard-educated lawyer, seemingly the model husband and father, was not accepted as suitable for the commander-in-chief role by some people. Why? Did he lack the education or experience? Did he not represent the same ideals of the democratic party as other democrats before this time? Or, let's be honest, was it the color of his skin?

His wife, Michelle, also a Harvard-educated lawyer, also faced many stereotypes wrongfully placed on black women. She was accused of being an angry black woman, harshly critiqued on her clothing choice, her body, and just overall given slack for her appearance.

After Barack Obama was elected, some white people in the south said they would rather be poor and white, in the lowest economic bracket in America, than be black—even if that blackness was the President of the United States. When Donald Trump ran and reintroduced the slogan *Make America Great Again*, the presumption was that it had racial connotations suggesting that it meant, *Get that black man out of the White House*. Others felt that the comment suggested division.

One thing also changed when both Presidents Obama and Trump were in office ... white supremacy increased, and America seemingly became more divided than it already was. Despite this, I do not believe it is really about politics but, instead, race. Yes, politics seemingly keep us divided, but this issue is bigger than politics. It is also bigger than race. This issue is spiritual—related to our hearts, minds, and souls.

Politics is something to hide behind because no one wants to be viewed as racist. Truth be told, racism is also something to hide behind, for those open enough to admit it. These matters of the heart are deeper than our time on earth. They are related to our souls and salvation. We have to get it right. The stakes are high and can be a matter of life or death, literally.

Fast-forward to August 2020, Presidential nominee Joe Biden selected Senator Kamala Harris as his running mate. I cannot recall previous elections where so much adverse attention and criticism was offered to the running mate and potential Vice President. As expected, she was immediately portrayed as the "angry black woman" and similar to Barack Obama, her blackness was questioned. Why is it that in success blackness is questioned, yet in adversity, the label is magnified and not questioned?

In 2020, the world also witnessed George Floyd take his last breath and his life be taken away from him. The aftermath caused a call to action. In the weeks following, we witnessed the removal of statues, the changing of names of schools and government buildings, removal of mascots and slogans, and the abandoning of titles and slurs that have racial connotations.

Some argue that the changes are too far-reaching and just not necessary. Is the gator bait chant a stretch, despite historical associations of the use of black babies as alligator bait? Is it ok to still wave the flag that represented the confederate states? Can the real estate arena continue to use certain terms and phrases such as master bedrooms?

Despite our opinions, we watched as many companies changed names, logos, and other insignia. Many companies made diversity statements, updated or created zero-tolerance policies, determined the need to hire or elevate diversity and inclusion personnel, closed their businesses for diversity trainings, and crafted immediate responses to show solidarity and support. While all of these steps are great, my hope is that they can be more substantive and not just for public relations purposes, and that there will be long-term action to reflect the statements.

One example of change that received media attention was NASCAR, Bubba Wallace, and the noose. In June 2020, NASCAR made a public statement to prohibit the display of confederate flags at their events and properties. Days after this statement, African American driver Bubba Wallace found a noose in his stall.

A noose, the knotted rope known to be used for lynching African Americans, is unacceptable. Was the presence of this noose a coincidence? Was the presence of this noose a threat or retaliation? There was controversy about when and how the noose got there, but even after hoax allegations, NASCAR confirmed that the noose was in fact present and that of 1684 stalls across 29 tracks, it was only found in the stall of Wallace.[45]

The noose example demonstrates that America is not post-racial and black Americans are often not viewed as equal, even in the workplace. After Floyd was killed, a post on social media called his death a public lynching, just without a noose. Others on social media began to make the correlation between forms of workplace oppression.

I read a post that said if someone can be lynched in broad daylight in front of bystanders with cameras, imagine what happens behind closed doors in human resource departments, in classrooms, medical offices, and other institutions. This post suggested that the issue is larger than defunding the police.

The issue exists not only within police departments. The change must be widespread. The many racial Facebook posts and comments suggest overwhelmingly that America is not post-racial. When Floyd's funeral was streamed live, many derogatory comments were made in the comment section under the stream, such as, "Just bury the criminal already." Others suggested that because he was a criminal, he did not deserve his photo on T-shirts, scholarships named after him, or the large murals.

America was built on the backs of slaves. Approximately 250 years of free slave labor have created generational wealth for some white Americans. Despite the argument by many that they do not own slaves, they may be beneficiaries of wealth that has been passed down for generations. Despite seemingly being free, African Americans are anywhere from 250 to 400 years behind, due to the unfair advantage and free labor provided from 1619–1865, and many after this period due to sharecropping and the prison system.

Fast-forward post-Thirteenth Amendment, African Americans, while free, left the plantations with absolutely nothing. Many then entered into sharecropping agreements, but they often found themselves further indebted to the master after unfair verbal contractual agreements.

Another topic often raised is whether black people having jobs and access makes them equal. Undeniably, black people are now educated and have desirable jobs. Black people are doctors, lawyers, and other professionals. A 2016 study reported that black women are now the most educated group in America.[46]

Despite black people having education and access to jobs, the representation is still disproportionate. Also, there are many issues with diversity and inclusion and retention in the workforce. Despite black people having educations and jobs, those in ownership and leadership positions are overwhelmingly white.

I'm not naïve enough to think class doesn't matter. My two little boys' experiences with a two-parent household with both parents having professional degrees and access to more resources will differ from another black boy their age who does not have the same resources or access. This doesn't mean that those other children's parents don't love them, but the difference in access is not attributable to love but to different resources.

I'm also not naïve enough to think that my boys will not have the negative stereotypes often attributed to black boys, despite their background, what their parents do, where we live, what they experience, or their education, and that must change.

In 1963, Martin Luther King Jr. delivered the famous "I Have a Dream" speech. Why is it that over fifty-five years later, I have the same dream as he did? I share his sentiments in dreaming about how I want to be judged and how I want my children to be perceived. I do not want them to be judged by the color of their skin but, instead, by the content of their character.

Black people may have good jobs, but it is not always equal. There are systematic barriers in place that persist. It is common for black people to experience the presumption of servitude in the workplace. Are you the receptionist? Now, there is nothing wrong with holding any job. I respect every individual and believe that every person deserves respect. But despite my law degree and license, tailored suit, and hard work, I have been asked if I'm the paralegal or court reporter, asked if I'm a student and not the professor.

I've been asked if I rent or own my home. You read that right. I have been asked if we own our downtown Minneapolis home, followed by the *what do you do* question? Is your husband a professional athlete? The presumptions, though perhaps not intentional, are offensive. I have been asked, "What do your parents do?" because surely they must be educated if I was able to achieve success and live in a gated community. Surely, I must have had a running start toward access to a professional degree.

These questions, fitting to microaggressions, are insulting and insensitive. This presumption also existed when I was in law school. A white male peer presumed I needed his help in a course after he scored the third-highest grade on a midterm exam. He did not know I had achieved the highest score on the midterm and could have offered him my assistance. I respectfully declined his assistance.

After the first semester, when all law students are ranked, I was in the top 10% of our class and this white male student was not. When I proceeded to get internship offers because of my class rank, he told me I was only getting jobs because of affirmative action and the need to fill a diversity quota. I asked him, "So it doesn't have anything to do with the fact that I am one of the top ten people in our class rank?" With a shocked look, he apologized for his faulty presumption.

Another common barrier is the job application process. It is not uncommon for a person to be perceived as a certain race or gender based on their name alone. The presumption is that LaQuisha Jenkins is a black woman and Karen Smith is a white woman. It is common to presume that Jamal Brown is a black man and Zack Anderson is a white man.

A 2017 Harvard article found that minority job applicants were more inclined to get interviews if they "whitened" the name on their resume or deleted experiences which reference their racial identities.[47] I had this discussion with a friend whose name almost assured that she was black. She asked if I would ever consider using my middle name, Michelle, to avoid the presumption that I was black. I told her not only did I like my name, but if a company was not interested in interviewing LaToya, the company likely would not be a good cultural fit for LaToya. As such, I refrained from using L. Michelle.

Discrimination also extends beyond race to gender. This same friend was concerned that she wasn't receiving callbacks because she was newly engaged. She felt that her engagement ring was prohibiting her from securing employment because the presumption was that a young newly married woman would inevitably want children. The presumption is that the children and maternity leave would interrupt her work productivity.

Despite resume and interview biases, should they exist, if a candidate is successful and hired, the racial biases may continue throughout their tenure. I would encourage every person to explore diversity, inclusion, and equity in their workplace. Many programs are in place to hire minorities from the lens of diversity, but do these programs have fundamental processes in place to truly make the minority worker feel included?

Are there mentors, managers, and leadership that reflect that diversity. Are trainings in place to educate everyone about bias, cultural competence, and microaggressions? What is the process to recruit, hire, and retain diverse candidates? Is that diversity equally distributed across multiple races, nationalities, and other groups, not just dominated by black people, white women, or members of the LGBT community? If there is not support, how can they succeed? If they don't feel a sense of community, they will not remain in the job or often will not excel in the job.

Added pressure is often placed on black people in the workforce. They are expected to be the voice for an entire group, are often subjected to subtle racial inequities, and are expected to perform under harsh conditions as the only minority, while presumptively fitting a one-size-fits-all stereotype about their race.

"All the black people come to you, right?" That is a question I was asked when I began to work at a university with a small minority population of African American students. Though innocent, the person asking the question naïvely felt that all black students would see me as a leader they could approach and confide in.

I responded, "No, actually, they do not, but why would they?"

You see, in the African American community, we understand that there could be a wide range of experiences. As such, the students, despite seeing my black face, did not know if my experience was similar enough to warrant the presumption of acceptance. I knew that if I did not intentionally initiate discussions, those students would not feel "safe" or open to developing a relationship with me. I understood that although black, many of the students may not have had experience with black people, let alone a professor of color.

Some of these students were biracial and despite black skin, were raised by their white parent and in all-white settings. Despite being black, they didn't see me as a resource and may not have felt that we had anything in common.

I worked at a law firm where a partner frequently engaged with me by using slang or Ebonics. He would greet me by saying, "Hey, girl" or "What up, T?" I did not like it. I did not do or say anything to suggest to him that this was ok, except have black skin, but I did not correct him. Statistics show that, overwhelmingly, black and minority associates do not excel in law firms despite being intelligent and capable. They are recruited and fill the diversity quota, but they often do not feel included and supported.

Associates are required to meet an annual billable-hour quota. To get the work to bill hours, you must have a personal and working relationship with a partner, typically developed from previous assignments or connections. Minority associates often express experiencing a lack of support or inclusion.

One example of bias in the workplace was reported in the *ABA Journal*. In this experimental study, partners were given identical legal briefs, with the only difference being the names of the authoring associate attorneys, one white and one black. The ratings for the black authored brief were lower rated, more spelling and grammar errors were pointed out, and, overall, more factual and writing errors were found than in the identical brief presumed to be authored by a white associate.[48] The black associate received harsh criticism about the brief and the white associate did not.

In law firms, the partner naturally mentors the person who looks like them, often another white male. On the flip side of the coin, the few minority partners are not always comfortable mentoring the sole minority associate because they don't want the misperception of showing favoritism to the other minority employee. This phenomenon is common and sometimes deters black people from publicly associating with one another.

When I first started working at a university, I decided to have an intentional lunch meeting targeting female students of color. The first meeting was held one month before spring graduation, and two of the black female graduating seniors introduced themselves to each other for the first time. How is it that on our small campus, these two minority students had never met?

I overheard their chatter.

One said, "I always wanted to say hello to you but didn't want to draw attention to our gathering."

Wow. In that moment, my heart broke. I doubt if most students on campus felt reservations about talking to another student of the same race solely because they were concerned about how their engaging would be perceived.

In addition to covert biases, it is common for the token black person to feel the pressure to not only perform on the job but to also be the voice for all minorities. Black people are expected to serve on diversity-related task forces and be the voice of reason for resolving all things race-related, in addition to performing their actual job.

One of my friends is the only African American partner in his large national law firm. He shared with me that he spent the weeks after the death of George Floyd in meeting after meeting discussing race, public statements that needed to be made, and the need to have listening sessions for black employees and clients. He explained how the process was exhausting and ultimately taking away from his ability to bill hours.

Diversity initiatives require time and work but are typically not considered when it's time for the annual review. He felt the need to point out the additional toll and load the diversity initiatives were taking on him now rather than explain his decline in billable hours at the end of the year when he falls short of his annual goals. These are only a few examples to explain why equality is not to be presumed. This does not even take into account the pay gap that persists with women and minorities.

One other related topic that impacts minorities in the work setting is code-switching. Code-switching is the requirement that minorities assimilate to majority white cultures when at work because of the fear that showing up as their true and authentic selves will not be acceptable. Some fear that showing up as themselves may be seen as a threat, but the real threat is the one that code-switching itself causes to diversity.

Code-switching causes people to have to suppress their identities and talk, walk, act, and react in a way that matches that of the white majority. Code-switching, in many instances, may be the difference between getting a job or not. In other cases, it may the difference between life and death. If a cop stops me, I will use a different tone and voice than I might use when talking to a close family member.

Code-switching may impact the way you dress and other cultural trends that you possess. Code-switching, not to be confused with professionalism, may cause me to second-guess how I wear my hair, the earrings I choose to wear, or the shoes I decide to wear. Despite how I might want to wear my hair, code-switching may cause me to be modest and wear my hair in a style more suitable to the majority group, as opposed to the natural kinky curl that grows from my scalp.

Code-switching causes you to have to know how to act among your family or neighborhood setting versus in the business setting. For me, that meant knowing how to "act" in the hood and boardroom. Why is that a requirement? When society suggests that only one culture, the majority, is proper, it often causes others to have to adjust their natural actions and reactions to that of the majority. Frankly, code-switching can be exhausting. It can also rob work settings of reflecting the true diversity of the workforce.

People say "You talk white" when someone speaks with proper diction. I am from Louisiana, a few miles south of New Orleans. I have been told, despite not living close to New Orleans in almost twenty years, that my accent is thick. My husband, a New Orleans native, also has a thick accent. We say y'all, yeah, baa-by, and other words common in New Orleans. I often felt like I needed to suppress this because I did not want this accent to be associated with a lack of education.

How is it that I can have coworkers with other accents that associate them with being educated, yet I felt the threat that my accent would associate me with a lack of education? I finally became comfortable in my voice. I know who I am. I know I am educated. I can only continue to be myself and hope that others will find value in that. I then shifted my focus away from trying to suppress my accent to intentionally not using phrases like uhm, ahh, or like and being more intentional about the use and clarity of my words.

Finally, one other threat is the definition of professionalism. Clean cut, clean-shaven, no ethnic hair, no flashy colors or accessories. I often accepted this strict attire as "professional" and not a way of suppressing cultural expressions or diversity. While I still believe that business attire should be tasteful, I am more open to what defines professionalism.

Discussion Questions

- Have you ever experienced or witnessed workplace bias? If yes, how did it make you feel?
- Have you ever had to code-switch?
- How should we define professionalism?

Question #9: Why can't I just ignore racism? I am not racist, and the topic makes me uncomfortable.

I don't want to say the wrong thing. I don't want to offend anyone. I want to ignore it and have it just simply go away. In a perfect world, this would be an acceptable response. The unfortunate reality is that racism is pervasive and just as it was created—and many believe it is a social construct—it will need to be dismantled and not ignored. I know the discussion is not comfortable for anyone, but it is necessary.

For my white friends who suggest that this discussion is uncomfortable, my response is simple ... I understand, but imagine not being able to avoid racism because of the color of your skin.... Even if racism makes me uncomfortable, I cannot avoid it. You see, when you are black or of color, you cannot avoid it. No matter who you are—your education, faith, background, or beliefs—what people see is your black skin. That in itself can be uncomfortable when you know it will lead to mistreatment or misjudgment for no reason at all. So yes, the discussion is admittedly uncomfortable for all, but it is necessary.

I encourage everyone to first, admit the discomfort, second, agree that the space is a safe place for vulnerability, and third, acknowledge that this process of growing from discomfort due to the unknown to being culturally competent is a process that requires work. The stretching may cause tension. The tension will ultimately cause a break. We want to break down biases and barriers.

Think about your educational journey. Whether you have a GED or PhD, what was the process? Did you feel nervous on the first day of school? How did you overcome the discomfort? Did you study and spend time with the course content? Did you ultimately overcome this discomfort? View overcoming the discomfort as it relates to race as similar to the discomfort on the first day of school.

Racial reconciliation must be intentional. It must be something that you want and are willing to work toward. The very act of engaging with this book suggests you want to make a change. At the end of this journey, your award may not be a diploma, but it will be freedom—freedom to engage with others and educate others as we journey toward racial reconciliation. That freedom and comfort is priceless.

As discussed in the Different Stages chapter, this journey has different stages, one of them being the fear zone. If you are uncomfortable with the discussions, you may be in good company in the fear zone, but as you work through this process, you will move from the learning to the growth zone! You have made the commitment and will boldly overcome the discomfort. You are reading this book, so you have chosen not to sit in fear. You are willing to stretch yourself beyond discomfort. You are willing to walk into the unknown.

If you stay in the discomfort you will keep a fixed mindset. If you accept that discomfort as normal but continue to push forward through the discomfort, you will have adopted a growth mindset. None of us are perfect. In growing, we may make mistakes, we may not know what to say, but we are willing to learn and grow ... together.

A previous student shared a racist experience with me. This biracial student had light brown skin, but her mother was African and her dad was white with blond hair and blue eyes. She told me that like many women, she was attracted to men that looked like her father. She also felt that black men were not attracted to her.

She began to date a white male student. She had spoken to his mother on the phone, but the mother presumed she was white. After a few months of dating, her boyfriend's mother found out she was black and told her son he could not date a black woman and she would not be accepted by their family. He broke up with her and told her the exact reason why. She was devastated and further saddened by the fact that he and his mother were Christians.

For this student, color and race issues were very real. She explained to me that she was one of five children from the same parents, and they all had different skin hues. She questioned, "What if my skin was white? Would his mother have accepted me but later had an issue when she discovered that my mother was black?"

Talking about race is often bigger than us. Even if you are not a racist, many people are, and they do not even realize they are. Their associations are that racists only commit blatant acts such as using the N-word or other hate crimes. Because they have a black friend or colleague, they may not believe they need racial reconciliation. But the very acts and associations that seem subtle can be racist in outcome. I wonder if this mother thought she was racist. Likely not, but when it hit home for her, perhaps deeper-rooted issues surfaced. Talking about race is more than just for ourselves.

Silence can speak volumes. In September 1963, the 16th Street Baptist Church was bombed by white supremacist and Klansmen, resulting in the killing of four African American girls between the ages of eleven and fourteen and injuring many others. The day after this tragic event,

Charles Morgan Jr. delivered a speech about race and prejudice to the Young Men's Business Club in Birmingham, Alabama. In this now historic speech, he posed the questions "Who did it? Who threw the bomb? Was it a Negro or a white? The answer should be 'We all did it.' Every last one of us is condemned for that crime and the bombing ... We all did it." This rings true when we are silent. Being uncomfortable yet silent when injustices occur is not acceptable.

We all have to step into the discomfort of talking about racism, whether we believe ourselves to be blatantly racist or not. Because of implicit biases and life experiences, this process toward racial reconciliation is a group effort! We cannot sit quietly in our comfort or privilege. There is too much at stake. I am so happy to be on this journey with you.

Discussion Questions

- Do you have any barriers preventing you from overcoming the fear associated with racism?
- How can you overcome the unknown?
- How can you help others overcome the discomfort of talking about race?

Question #10: Why protest? It doesn't work. Surely there is a more peaceful way to address these issues.

Protests are expressions of disapproval and are constitutionally protected via the First Amendment. Before discussing protest, we must differentiate between three distinct groups: protestors, rioters, and looters. The water is muddied because rioters and looters usually are in attendance to protest and its often a challenge to differentiate who is present for what reason.

The simple presence of rioters and looters does not negate the protections afforded to peaceful protestors. My disappointment with rioters and looters is that their presence often detracts from the reason protestors are out and attention is drawn to any damage caused by rioters or looters. The damage significantly overshadows the message that protestors are present to send.

When peacefully done, protests can and do send the intended message. Protestors often feel that they don't have other options. If there is a message to be heard and simply talking does not get attention, protestors will take to the streets to have their voices heard. We are reminded of this when reflecting on the life and death of civil rights leader, politician, and former House of Representative member, Congressman John Lewis.

Congressman Lewis, known for his connection to Dr. Martin Luther King Jr. and activist work, dedicated his life to racial equality and justice. We are reminded of the power of protests in his famous quote, "Never, ever be afraid to make some noise and get in good trouble, necessary trouble." Protests are good and necessary.

In 2016, well-known ex-football player and activist Colin Kaepernick received slack for kneeling during the national anthem. The criticism ultimately resulted in him losing his career. His reason for kneeling was to silently protest police brutality. Many were offended that he would choose to kneel during the national anthem and suggested there must be another way for him to send his message.

Some also questioned why he would choose to kneel and considered his actions dishonoring not only to the flag but to the military and veterans. Specifically, some people state that kneeling is offensive because their grandfathers fought in the war or they have family members who currently serve or are veterans. They fail to realize that black soldiers also fought in the same war and many black people also have military families, both active and veterans.

Many of these same soldiers fought and came back to an America that still disregarded the value of their lives merely because of the color of their skin. Many of these black veterans understand exactly why Kaepernick took a knee. In a social media debate, one person said that kneeling was a direct violation of the flag code. The counterargument stated that the very constitution is not followed as all men are not treated like they are created equally.

Kaepernick's quiet protest did not include the opportunity for rioters and looters, but many chose not to focus on the very reason he said he knelt. Instead, attention was shifted from his intended message toward suggesting that he was disrespecting the American flag and veterans. The attention he hoped to gain was an awareness about police brutality and, in turn, call for police and criminal justice reform. His kneeling went so much deeper than simply disrespecting a flag, but many could not get past the flag to hear out his reasoning. The alternative to his quiet kneeling, which many still take issue with, is the protests in streets around the world.

Protests are not new. In fact, protests are not limited to black America. Although I will focus on the civil rights movement and the result of its protests, historically, protests were related to many other significant historical events, including, but not limited to, The Boston Tea Party, The French Revolution, or even the Suffragettes Movement.

The civil rights movement was not the first of its kind and was not the last. A similar movement followed in Northern Ireland, known as The Troubles, and Apartheid took place in South Africa, leading up to Nelson Mandela becoming the country's first black president.

Some have compared the recent 2020 protests to the civil rights movement. During the civil rights movement, the most successful outcomes were the result of protests. The first example is the Civil Rights Act of 1957. This Act didn't result from silence but, instead, from extreme measures, including bus boycotts, marches, protests, lawsuits, lobbying, and other measures to be heard.

The March on Washington for Jobs and Freedoms, which took place in August 1963, was known as one of the largest civil rights gatherings in US history. This protest is known for the famous "I Have a Dream" speech Dr. Martin Luther King Jr. memorably delivered. The media captured this massive protest and gathering of over 250,000 people, and the protest resulted in further legislation.

The Civil Rights Act of 1964 followed. This Act was more comprehensive and extended the equal rights declared in 1957 to prevent segregation in public places such as hotels, restaurants, theaters, parks, and others. The results from 1957 and 1964 suggest that protests do, in fact, work. The civil rights movement victories include the overruling of Jim Crow segregation and the passing of specific amendments, acts, and other laws. This Act also resulted in the creation of the Equal Employment Opportunity Commission (EEOC). Also stemming from the demands for fair employment practices was the passage of the Voting Rights Act of 1965.

Protests can and do work, and history supports this. Protests are not outdated. In 2020, many have asked why people are protesting. If protests lead to rioting and looting, is it worth it? Why risk the potential destruction of your community? The response to these questions should be "Why do people feel that they have no other choice besides protesting?" As a result of the May and June 2020 protests, here is an abbreviated list of specific actions that have followed:

- The officers involved in the George Floyd shooting were arrested and charged.
- Additional protests took place around the globe to address racism, police brutality, and other forms of inequities, including on every continent except Antarctica.
- The Minneapolis City Council banned the use of chokeholds and required officers to report and intervene when they see excessive force being used.
- Many other cities took action, including, but not limited to, the following: Dallas adopted a duty to intervene rule and New Jersey updated the use of force guidelines.

- The Minneapolis City Council proposed police reform, including defunding the police departments. Other states took similar actions, including Maryland forming a police reform working group, and Los Angeles reduced the LAPD budget.
- Corporations have made public statements, including instituting zero-tolerance policies against racism or discrimination.
- The Justice in Policing Act of 2020 was introduced, which would prevent unannounced police raids and no-knock warrants.
- Confederate and other statues of those with racist histories have been removed.
- Buildings have been renamed.
- CEOs have resigned due to racially insensitive comments and actions.
- Products have been rebranded.
- The street leading to the White House was named Black Lives Matter Plaza.
- Discussions are taking place and hearts are being changed.

Peaceful protests absolutely work, especially in the information age we live in. Social media platforms allow for organizing and instant information spread. During the civil rights movement, despite limited media platforms, the responses to peaceful protestors were also given attention and favorable responses when the news coverage showed real-time footage of the harsh treatment that was happening to peaceful protestors.

Protests are effective, but their purpose and power should not be overshadowed by often independent rioters or looters that mistakenly appear to be related. As long as there are injustices, protests remain powerful tools. My favorite result from the recent protests is the open and honest discussions that are now taking place, leading to a change of heart for many. Those discussions are leading to education. People are listening, learning, and becoming Bold! The protests led to this book and may have led you to this book! For that, I am forever thankful. I will end this chapter with two powerful quotes.

When injustice becomes law, resistance becomes duty. (Thomas Jefferson)

Power concedes nothing without a demand. It never did and it never will. Find out just what any people will quietly submit to and you have found out the exact measure of injustice and wrong which will be imposed upon them, and these will continue till they are resisted with either words or blows, or with both. The limits of tyrants are prescribed by the endurance of those whom they oppress. In the light of these ideas, Negroes will be hunted at the North, and held and flogged at the South so long as they submit to those devilish outrages, and make no resistance, either moral or physical. Men may not get all they pay for in this world; but they must certainly pay for all they get. If we ever get free from the oppressions and wrongs heaped upon us, we must pay for their removal. We must do this by labor, by suffering, by sacrifice, and if needs be, by our lives and the lives of others. (Frederick Douglass)

Discussion Questions

- What are some ways you have directly or indirectly been impacted by protests?
- Do you believe protests should be protected by the First Amendment?
- What are some ways we can address injustices?

11

BE BOLD

Learn to do right; seek justice. Defend the oppressed. Take up the cause of the fatherless; plead the case of the widow.

—Isaiah 1:17

This book will not solve the racism problem. Racism is a sin problem and evil will continue to persist. The goal of this book is to start a dialogue toward a broader solution. I pray that you have had an ah-ha moment while reading this book. One discussion at a time, we can improve our circles, both our social and professional circles, and ultimately get at the root of the systematic and internal racism and oppression. While we may never wipe out racism, we can make it unacceptable ... Not the norm ... Not something deeply embedded, and we can continue to work toward dismantling racism.

We must educate ourselves about racism. We cannot ignore racism and its impact. A lack of tolerance needs to be the new normal. We need these collective dialogues to see systemic changes and ensure that racism is ultimately dismantled. Continue to open your heart and mind and Be Bold!

Now that we have reached this stage of the book, I encourage you to reflect on the Pretest from the Roadmap for This Journey chapter. Have your thoughts about your answers changed? Have your opinions shifted? Has there been any measurable growth? By the very nature of the questions, some of them cannot change, but have your overall feelings about the question and your answers changed? We must acknowledge racism and intentionally work toward dismantling it.

You are *bold*! You are powerful. You are a resource! You are intentional. You are a leader. You are a changemaker. If you desire to continue to grow toward eliminating racism, here are some things you can do daily:

- Speak up when you experience or witness something inappropriate and racially motivated, every single time. Be the voice!
- Continue to have difficult discussions in all circles of your life: at home, at work, at school, at church, with your friends and family.
- Continue to learn and grow and strengthen your understanding of racism.
- Continue to examine yourself, acknowledge biases, attitudes, and microaggressions, and work toward personal improvement.
- Support and speak about anti-racist policies within your community, job, and other circles.

- Pay attention to the media, slogans, and offensive terms and actions, and call them out.
- Volunteer or financially support organizations designed to combat racism.
- Be a change agent! Be Bold!

If we want there to be a change, we must change. My hope is that we can get to a place where racism no longer has to be a part of the narrative. Until then, we must be *Bold*!

Let us all hope that the dark clouds of racial prejudice will soon pass away and the deep fog of misunderstanding will be lifted from our fear drenched communities, and in some not too distant tomorrow the radiant stars of love and brotherhood will shine over our great nation with all their scintillating beauty.

—Yours for the cause of Peace and Brotherhood, Martin Luther King, Jr.[49]

We can be better together! We are better together! Go and...

BE BOLD!

Acknowledgments

If you want to go quickly, go alone. If you want to go far, go together.

—African Proverb

First, I give all honor and praise to my Lord and Savior Jesus Christ who is the head of my life. His grace is sufficient and his mercy endureth forever (Ps. 118). Second, I would like to give thanks and honor to my husband for always being my biggest supporter, life partner, the leader of our family, and best friend. Thank you for your patience and grace with me as I jumped knee-deep into this writing project during an already challenging time in our world.

To my children, Grayson and Garrison, thank you for motivating me to always be my very best. Thanks for challenging me and stretching me in every way possible. I am thankful that God entrusted me with being your mother. I am humbled and forever grateful.

I am also incredibly thankful for my tribe, which includes my immediate family and my friends, who I call my "framily." The daily calls and texts are appreciated and keep me grounded in my faith and, ultimately, the essence of who I am. Thank you for your support and daily encouragement.

To my colleagues, thanks for the genuine support and intellectually stimulating discussions and opportunities to grow. Iron sharpens iron, and I am grateful for my work family.

To my social media family and friends, thank you for your support. The likes, shares, and personal messages have been heartfelt and motivating.

To everyone who took the time to assist me with this process toward publication, thank you! Thank you for reading my drafts, hearing my heart, and helping me publish this book with ease.

To my readers, thank you for boldly taking this journey with me! The best is yet to come.

About the Author

LaToya J. Burrell currently serves as Dean of Graduate Education and Accreditation at North Central University in Minneapolis, Minnesota. She has taught many different subjects, including business law, leadership, ethics, and other business-related courses. She has taught Professional Responsibility at Mitchell Hamline School of Law and has served in various capacities in the legal community. She serves on multiple institutional committees and is also a Higher Learning Commission Peer Reviewer and the institution's Accreditation Liaison Officer.

LaToya is an attorney licensed to practice law in Louisiana and Minnesota and has previously devoted her practice to bankruptcy law and complex litigation. Her research interest includes higher education law, Americans with Disabilities law, leadership, and racial reconciliation. She believes in the power of mentoring and serves as the American Mock Trial Association's coach. She is on the board of directors at People Serving People, Inc. and loves volunteering her time

A Louisiana native, wife, mother, and leader, LaToya lives in Minneapolis, Minnesota with her husband and two sons. For more information or to contact LaToya, please visit www.theboldlatoyaburrell.com.

Endnotes

Many of the references include websites, which were active at the date of publication. The author does not hold responsibility for post-publication changes or deletions. All Bible references appear in the Holy Bible, New International Version (NIV) translation.

[1] Joles, D. "Minneapolis Police Name First Black Chief in Wake of Shooting." August 21, 2017. Retrieved from https://www.nbcnews.com/news/nbcblk/minneapolis-police-name-first-black-chief-wake-shooting-n793956.

[2] Drucker, Peter F. *Managing in Turbulent Times*. 1980. New York: Harper & Row.

[3] Strong, James. *Strong's Exhaustive Concordance of the Bible*. Abingdon Press, 1890.

[4] Benner, J. *Introduction to Ancient Hebrew*. Retrieved from www.ancient-hebrew.org.

[5] King Jr., M.L. *Love in Action* Sermon. April 3, 1960.

[6] Ackerman, C. "What is Self-Awareness and Why is it Important? +5 Ways to Increase It." April 4, 2020. Retrieved from https://positivepsychology.com/self-awareness-matters-how-you-can-be-more-self-aware/.

[7] Chakraborty, R. "The US Medical System is Still Haunted by Slavery." December 7, 2017. Retrieved from https://www.vox.com/health-

care/2017/12/7/16746790/health-care-black-history-ine-quality.

[8] Madison, J. "The Writings of James Madison." The Journal of the Constitutional Convention, Part I, 1902.

[9] *Dred Scott v. Sandford*, 60 US 393 (1856).

[10] Duvernay, A. & Moran, J. *13th*. 2016.

[11] https://www.juneteenth.com/.

[12] Maxorious, C. *The 1921 Tulsa Race Massacre will soon be a part of the curriculum for Oklahoma Schools.* February 20, 2020.

[13] Moore, A., & Gibbons, D. *Watchmen*. 1987. New York: Warner Books.

[14] Cane, C. "Not Just Tulsa: Race Massacres That Devastated Black Communities in Rosewood, Atlanta, and Other American Cities." May 31, 2020. Retrieved from https://www.bet.com/news/national/2019/12/17/not-just-tulsa--five-other-race-massacres-that-devastated-black.html

[15] Retrieved from https://www.britannica.com/topic/black-code.

[16] History.com Editors. "Black Codes." Updated October 10, 2019. Retrieved from https://www.history.com/topics/black-history/black-codes.

[17] "The Fleur-de-lis." Retrieved from https://web.archive.org/web/20170513022919/http://www.uark.edu/ua/nc/ClarinetCollections/Heinrich%20Gehring/Fleur-de-Lis/Fleur-de-Lis.htm.

[18] *Plessy v. Ferguson*, 163 US 537 (1895).

Endnotes

[19] *Brown v. Board of Education*, 347 US 483 (1954).

[20] CNN. "Civil Rights Timeline." February 21, 2007. Retrieved from https://www.cnn.com/2006/EDUCATION/01/31/extra.civil.rights.timeline/index.html.

[21] King Jr., M.L. "The Other America." March 14, 1968. Retrieved from https://www.gphistorical.org/mlk/mlk-speech/.

[22] SurgeryRedesign.com. "Becoming Anti-Racist." Retrieved from https://umich.app.box.com/s/d1zl3r2dlso7gs76wjfybv9z52m397ho.

[23] Angelou, M. *And Still I Rise*, 1978.

[24] Morrison, T. *Beloved: A Novel*. New York: Knopf, 1987.

[25] Twin Cities PBS. *Jim Crow of the North*. Documentary. February 25, 2019.

[26] King Jr., M. L. "I Have a Dream." Speech presented at the March on Washington for Jobs and Freedom, Washington, DC, August 1968.

[27] King Jr., M. L. "Letter from the Birmingham Jail." San Francisco: Harper San Francisco.

[28] Retrieved from https://www.naacpldf.org/ldf-celebrates-60th-anniversary-brown-v-board-education/significance-doll-test/.

[29] McIntosh, P. *White Privilege: Unpacking the Invisible Knapsack*. 1988.

[30] "Thomas Jefferson and Sally Hemings: A Brief Account." Retrieved from

https://www.monticello.org/thomas-jefferson/jefferson-slavery/thomas-jefferson-and-sally-hemings-a-brief-account/.

31 *The Today Show.* "Black Descendants of Thomas Jefferson Speak Out at Monticello." July 6, 2020. Retrieved from https://www.youtube.com/watch?v=cely0c18Kak.

32 Perkins, J. and Waddles, K. *One Blood: Parting Words to the Church on Race and Love* (Chicago: Moody Publishers, 2018), 45.

33 Retrieved from https://www.merriam-webster.com/dictionary/racism.

34 Goldin, C. and Rouse, C. *Blind" Orchestra Auditions Reduce Sex-Biased Hiring and Increase the Number of Female Musicians.* September 2000.

35 Harris, O. and Pawlowski, A. *If you're Black and a woman, nothing else is visible.* July 20, 2020.

36 Ibid.

37 https://implicit.harvard.edu/implicit/takeatest.html.

38 https://idiinventory.com/about-us/.

39 Retrieved from https://kstp.com/news/conversations-about-racism-and-the-road-to-equality-understanding-racism-july-15-2020/5793654/?cat=1.

40 *Dred Scott v. Sandford*, 60 US 393 (1856).

41 https://www.thecrownact.com/.

42 https://blacklivesmatter.com/about/.

43 Long, H. and Van Dam, A. *The Black-White Economic Divide is As Wide as It Was in 1968.* June 4, 2020.

[44] Killough, A. and Lavandera, E. *This Small Louisiana Parish Has the Highest Death Rate Per Capita For Coronavirus in the Country,* CNN April 16, 2020. Retrieved from https://www.cnn.com/2020/04/15/us/louisiana-st-john-the-baptist-coronavirus/index.html.

[45] George, P. "NASCAR Says It Wants to Move on From the Noose. Its Fans Must Do the Same." June 26, 2020. Retrieved from https://www.thedrive.com/opinion/34385/nascar-says-it-wants-to-move-on-from-the-noose-its-fans-must-do-the-same.

[46] Osborne, S. "Black Women Become Most Educated Group in US." June 3, 2016. Retrieved from https://www.independent.co.uk/news/world/americas/black-women-become-most-educated-group-in-us-a7063361.html.

[47] Schwantes, M. "Harvard Study Says Minority Job Candidates Are 'Whitening' Their Resumes When Looking for Jobs." Retrieved from https://www.inc.com/marcel-schwantes/why-minority-job-applicants-mask-their-race-identities-when-applying-for-jobs-according-to-this-harvard-study.html.

[48] Weiss, D. "Partners in Study Gave Legal Memo a Lower Rating When Told the Author Wasn't White." April 21, 2014. Retrieved from https://www.abajournal.com/news/article/hypothetical_legal_memo_demonstrates_unconscious_biases.

[49] King Jr., M. L. "Letter from the Birmingham Jail." San Francisco: Harper San Francisco.